believe?

charlotte scanlon-gambill

Abundant Life Publishing

Abundant Life Publishing
Wapping Road, Bradford
West Yorkshire BD3 0EQ

Charlotte Scanlon-Gambill has asserted her right under the Copyright,
Designs and Patents Act, 1988, to be identified as Author of this work.

First Published in 2005

Printed by:
Interprint Creative Solutions
Market Flat Lane, Knaresborough
North Yorkshire HG5 9JA

www.interprint-ltd.co.uk

British Library Cataloguing in Publication Data
A catalogue record for this book is available from the British Library

ISBN 0-9538516-6-4

dedication

To my husband, Steve.

We have been on this journey through life together now for over thirteen years and every day I love you more.

I have never once heard you doubt God; your belief in him is rock solid.

You give the gift of belief to everyone you meet. I have seen you transform the lives of young people by believing in them.

Steve, you have believed with me, believed for me and believed in me. I love you and dedicate this book to you.

Charl

contents

Chapter 1 - believe?

Chapter 2 - the gift of belief

Chapter 3 - believers are doers

Chapter 4 - first followers

Chapter 5 - can't or won't?

Chapter 6 - much entrusted

Chapter 7 - the culture of asking

Chapter 8 - lend me your loaf

Chapter 9 - your time is up

We need a belief that has
been somewhere, that has
done something,
that has given us a
story to tell.

CHAPTER 1

believe?

So you are saved, you're part of God's family and a child of the king. You are set free, planted in God's House and are connected to your higher plan. You have a destiny, a future full of the promises of God, and you are called, set apart and victorious. Maybe this is what you say, but is it what you really believe?

Many Christians have become highly skilled at eloquently expressing God's truth, they can memorise scriptures and recite whole parables. Yet they have reduced the awesome life-changing principles that these stories hand them to information, rather than something that can transform their lives. God's truth for these Believers is firmly in their head but has not been embedded into their hearts. It is more of a theory than a reality in their lives.

Today, you may know the promises of God. You may even be the proud owner of a promise-box, you may have the 'I can do all things through Christ' fridge magnet and enjoy deep, daily devotionals with friends. But the question still needs to be asked, how much of what you know is a reality to you? Where is it lived out and experienced? Has your belief been road tested?

What you 'say' you believe may sound very impressive, even inspiring, but if your belief isn't tested it is like a shiny car sitting in the showroom of your life. It is just a prized possession that you admire but have never actually used. That car brings with it a whole range of options and possibilities about journeys you could take and places you could go. But unless it is road tested you will never find out what it can really do.

Some people just don't want to try out their faith; they don't want to risk damaging the paintwork so they leave it in the comfort and safety of the car showroom. They attend church, they believe 'in' God, but do they really 'believe' God's Word? They claim his promises over their lives yet they are not doing anything to make those promises a reality. They are living with the gear stick of their faith in neutral and the handbrake firmly on.

Surely there is more to our faith than that. We signed up for more than just a belief, we signed up for living the adventure that Christ died for. We owe it to ourselves, our families and those in our world to have a faith that has been tried out on the open road. A faith that is real and even has a few bumps and scrapes on it from the tests it has been through. A faith that has taken us through some experiences and has given us a story to tell. We need a belief that has been somewhere and that has done something. So, you may be reading this as a leader, a pastor, part of a worship team, a long standing church member, and someone committed to serving God with all your heart, but there is still something lacking. Maybe you are still in the showroom and are being held back by unbelief. If we are honest, we all have times when belief is lacking in our world so we all have some work to do.

UNBELIEVING BELIEVERS

In 2 Corinthians we are warned against being yoked with unbelievers: *'Do not be yoked together with unbelievers ... What does a believer have in common with an unbeliever?'* [1]

This scripture is a clear warning to stay away from wrongly attaching our lives to the unsaved. It is urging us to examine how involved and how entangled we let our lives become with people who do not share our core beliefs and values. When you yoke your life to another person's life, it is more than a casual acquaintance and deeper than a passing friendship. It's a level of relationship that forms an attachment and says, 'I am journeying through life with you'.

That is why it is so important that we are thorough in deciding who we yoke our lives to. We cannot afford to only be guarded about yoking ourselves to the unsaved and be cautious in our relationships with backsliders. You can't read 2 Corinthians 6:14 and just avoid one type of unbeliever!

We have an epidemic of 'unbelieving believers' on our hands and I have found over the years that many of the worst infected people are saved and seated in church every weekend. Their doubt and negativity is just as hazardous, if not more, than that of the unchurched who don't claim to know any better. Unbelief eats away at their faith and it will infect the lives of those healthy Believers who are yoked to them. Unbelief is debilitating, it erodes confidence, restricts progress, chokes faith, closes doors and drowns possibilities in a sea of negativity. So we need to get more radical about who we join ourselves to, because an unbelieving Believer will shrink your life and seriously deteriorate your spiritual life span.

We must refuse to join our lives to anyone, saved or unsaved, who is a carrier of the disease of unbelief. Too often we yoke our lives with other Christians and assume that because we are on the same journey we are heading in the same direction. Yet I have met many Christians whose destination is unbelief and if you attach your life to theirs, then your destination will be the same. In Amos it says 'Do two people walk hand in hand if they aren't going to the same *place?*' [2] If we believe this verse then we need to wise up and be more selective about the company we keep.

I love to exercise. Every day I run on my treadmill and I regularly go walking with my mum. We walk for miles together and the purpose of the exercise is usually to work off the cheesecake we ate the night before! When we set off we are in total agreement that this is not a stroll, it is not about enjoying the scenery but is a jog to burn off the calories. However, my husband on a sunny afternoon last summer suggested that we went for a walk. I assumed he understood that for me, the primary purpose of any walk was exercise. We soon got into a disagreement because I was exasperated by his meandering pace, the fact he had worn flip flops and that he was in no hurry to go anywhere. We were at cross purposes because I had set off presuming he also wanted to run, that he would be wearing his trainers and be looking forward to working up a sweat. We should have agreed on this before we left the house because that day our purpose and therefore our pace were both different.

Right now many people are trying to keep in step with others whose pace is completely different to theirs. They are unequally yoked together, so frustration is mounting from both sides. So when people join you, make it clear to them where you are going and check out whether their final destination is belief or unbelief.

DEEP SEA BELIEF

In this book I want to challenge you to consider whether you are a believing Believer or an unbelieving Believer. Maybe you have never thought about this before, so ask yourself the question, 'do I believe?' Are you totally and utterly convinced about what you believe and if so where is that conviction being worked out? Or are you playing it safe, are you a conformist who is unwilling to take a risk to advance the cause that you claim to believe so strongly in? Do you doubt you are capable of actually doing what you pray and sing about?

A while ago my husband bought me a beautiful new watch. It's a gorgeous piece of jewellery and I will treasure it for a long time. My watch came with all kinds of guarantees and promises, one of them being that it is water resistant. Its warranty even assures me it can be taken deep sea diving. So my watch would be fine if I ever got the urge to do it, but I'm not sure whether I would survive! So why is it that I still take my watch off when I have a shower and I wouldn't dream of wearing it when I go for a swim at the gym? Although the information on the warranty is there for me to read, and I know this is what the watch was designed to do, I still don't dare put it to the test.

And that is the exact same problem so many of us have when it comes to believing God. We have the promises and guarantees of his incredible Word which tell us how much we can do through him and with him. Yet so often we don't believe it enough to give it a try! We have deep sea potential yet we live life in the shallow end. If you are keeping your believing tucked safely away like I did with my watch, then it is time to put it on, take the plunge and go deep sea diving! You will only ever be totally convinced of what it can do if you put it to the test.

BELIEVE IT OR NOT?

One of the easiest ways to identify a believing Believer from an unbelieving Believer is to look at the way they act, speak and think. You will find unbelief thinly veiled in a cynical comment; you will find it in the question that is dressed up as a concern. It can come in various disguises and we need to work on our ability to recognise the symptoms. Unbelieving Believers have mastered the art of camouflage because they want to blend in. They are the chameleons of church life who change their colour to suit the opinions of those around and prevent drawing attention to themselves. They are not convinced enough about what they really believe on certain issues to stand out from the crowd and feel awkward when put under the spotlight or questioned about it. Unbelief is often so subtle we can miss it in our own lives and in the lives of those around us. It can infect your life gradually without you realising it, so you need to be careful you are not a carrier.

When I challenged my own life about this whole concept of believing I found I had some work to do because the easy part is saying we believe in something. But if you really do believe there will be some evidence.

So let's consider a few of the promises that we say we believe and see what they should look like when you take them off the page and apply them to your everyday life. Just to get started, look at the statements below and ask yourself, do you believe them or not?

It says in Genesis that '*God created man in his own image.*' [3] But do you really believe that? Do you believe that you are special; that God gave you his own DNA when he made you? If so, why then do you have such a problem about the way you look and why are you constantly comparing yourself to other people? If you believed it, you would be confident in your appearance and have a good sense of self worth because you are created in God's image. You would even invest in your health and well being because knowing you are God's handiwork means you will take care of yourself. Can you put your hand on your heart and say you believe that you are a masterpiece of creation, that you believe you are an original created by God for a unique and special purpose? Do you believe it or not?

It says, '*seek first his kingdom and his righteousness, and all these things will be given to you as well.*' [4] If you believe it, why then do you spend a minimal amount of time seeking his kingdom, being instead preoccupied by spending the majority of your time building and improving your own world? You are always working on adding to your list of belongings and adding to your list of possessions but when did you last spend time adding to his kingdom? Are you also adding to the number of people who will populate heaven by sharing your faith, giving your life away and laying down your priorities in order to pursue his? If you believe that God will bless your world with everything you will ever need for your life, then it will show up in the way you manage your time and what your priorities are. Do you believe it or not?

It says in Philippians that, 'the peace of God, which transcends all understanding, will guard your hearts and your minds in Christ Jesus.' [5] Do you really believe that you can have peace that surpasses understanding? It is such an incredible promise from God, but if you believe it, why then are you having trouble sleeping at night? If you are stressed out about your job, your finances, your ministry, your children or any area of your life, then you are not truly believing and standing on God's peace. So many times when I have gone through situations that have brought unrest into my world I have had to make a decision to trust in God and allow his peace that surpasses understanding to still my heart and silence my questions. And you can have it too. It just depends on whether you believe it or not!

Scripture also says, '*Who of you by worrying can add a single hour to his life? Since you cannot do this very little thing, why do you worry about the rest?*' [6] What does this look like in your life? Because if you believe you don't need to worry, you won't panic when things go wrong. You won't stop giving financially because you have a problem with your cash flow, and you won't get mad with God saying, 'Why me?' every time life doesn't go your way. You will stop using your energy on worry and believe God's Word. Do you believe it or not?

THE LITMUS TEST

I don't remember much about science at school but one experiment I can recall was called the litmus test. We would place litmus paper in a liquid and watch as it rapidly changed colour to show you whether or not the liquid was acidic or alkaline. In the same way, circumstances are the litmus test of the belief levels in your life. They clearly show where you are at and for many people they give an indication of how low their belief levels have become. It's not the amount you know that will get you through, but the quality and depth of what you believe that ultimately counts.

Several years ago at a training event for youth leaders, someone told me that if I was serious about my faith I should read my Bible from cover to cover, over and over again. That advice was flawed because I needed the Bible to be far more than information. The truth of God's Word had to become real to me and for that to happen I had to stop trying to impress people with how much I had read. Instead, I needed to slow down and take the time to understand and apply it to my life. Now, I sometimes take a month to think about a particular verse because I have realised that believing comes through understanding, experiencing and trying out what I have read. You need to let God's truth saturate your life because this will boost your belief levels and help you pass any test heading your way. It's not 'what' you know but 'who' you know that matters.

Right now your circumstances are giving you a litmus test reading. You may not have seen them like that before but I am encouraging you to look again at the challenges of your life. What are they telling you about what you believe? Let your circumstances work for you, let them give you a reading of where you are at on the road map of your life. Maybe you thought you were a lot further on than you are.

I faced one such litmus test several years ago when I was told that there was little chance I would ever be able to have children. In times like these our believing is shown up for what it really is. Only having a knowledge about God would never have sustained me through that; I had to know God, I had to know his love for me and know that he wanted the best for me. Sometimes Believers can get all hot and bothered declaring scriptures over their circumstances while they hold unbelief in their hearts. It just doesn't work like that, these scriptures need to be real in your life. The proof of this will become no more apparent than in the face of a challenge.

That day as we sat in the hospital consultants office reeling from the news we had been given, my husband Steve and I had a choice to make that would be a defining moment in our lives. Together we decided to believe God, we decided to believe his Word more than the word of the doctors. We decided to believe more in his ability to bless us than our inability to have a child. We knew that God wanted to bless us and felt that our desire to have our own family was God given, so we refused to let go of our dream.

We started fertility treatment which meant endless trips to the hospital, check-ups and daily injections. Every time the pregnancy test result came back negative we had to hold on to God's Word.

It was the first night of Cherish 2002, our annual women's conference, which I was hosting. The main auditorium was packed out with women and there was an amazing sense of expectancy in the atmosphere. I was just getting ready to go out and preach when I found out that our seventh cycle of fertility treatment had failed. We were only allowed eight attempts on the fertility programme we were on and now we were down to our last chance! That night I had a choice. I could either go back to my office and cry, or I could smile, walk through the door and start the conference. When I preached that night I spoke with everything in my heart. I wasn't trying to talk myself into it, or speaking through gritted teeth just to get through, I wanted to preach a message that would encourage all those women who had travelled from across the globe to be with us. That night I expressed my believing by what I did, I trusted in God and his plan for my life and the very next month I conceived.

Today we have our beautiful daughter, Hope Cherish, who is everything we dreamed of and more, and is a God-given gift. We chose her name because she represents what we believe. The hope we have is not just a statement, it is a tested, lived out action and I know that it was choosing to be believing Believers, even when our circumstances said different, that made this miracle possible.

So let me ask, what does believing look like in your world? Do you have stories where your faith has carried you through situations, where your belief in God has been a stronger pull on your world than your circumstances or what the unbelieving Believers around you are saying? If as you read this you are facing relationship breakdown, do you believe he is the restorer of your soul? If you are facing unemployment do you believe that he is your provider? If you are sick do you believe that he is your healer? If faced with bereavement, do you believe he is your comforter? And if it's failure, do you believe that he is the lifter of your head? The choice is yours, believe it or not!

I could fill an entire book and more just telling you about the amazing things God has for you and the awesome promises that are yours if only you would believe. But unless you choose to believe it will make no difference to your life. You need to remember that we are all on a journey of believing, we all have areas that God will stretch us and challenge us in. So, if you know there are things you need to improve on then be encouraged, because when we fall short the problem is always from our end not God's, which means we can change!

You can become a believing Believer in every area of your life. How? Well, my advice is to read on!

[1] 2 Corinthians 6:14-15

[2] Amos 3:3   The Message

[3] Genesis 1:27

[4] Matthew 6:33

[5] Philippians 4:7

[6] Luke 12:25-26

Believing in Someone
is an incredible gift
you can give to
their world.

CHAPTER 2

the gift of belief

When I was growing up I was not the most athletic of girls. I preferred doing the 'arty' stuff and to sit chatting with my friends! I'd rather have been doing anything other than PE – Physical Education. I hated it so much that I have to confess that I used to forge sick notes from my mum to get me out of it!

The thing I hated most about PE was that you had to stand in line while someone picked teams. I'd stand in line, and I'd wait, and I'd wait until there was no-one else left and the teacher would say, 'Who wants Charlotte?'
'I suppose we'll have her', was the unenthusiastic response! My team mates would then send me off into the far corners of the school playing field in case the ball headed that way. I'd say, 'Is this far enough out?'

And they'd say, 'No, go further, further,' just in case I embarrassed them by trying to catch the ball. I would end up so far back in the out-field that I wouldn't even know when the game had finished; someone would have to come and fetch me to tell me they had gone in to get changed!

I was never chosen to be part of the team, no-one thought I was good enough and that might be how you feel. We can often take too much notice of whether other people have chosen and included us. You may feel like that at different times in your life, feeling that you are the one who is always left out. You may feel that no-one believes in you. But God has chosen you, and he doesn't look at you through human eyes. He can see your hidden explosive potential and you are on his team because you have a unique part to play. Jesus said of his disciples, *'I no longer call you servants, because a servant does not know his master's business. Instead, I have called you friends, for everything that I learned from my Father I have made known to you. You did not choose me, but I chose you and appointed you to go and bear fruit - fruit that will last.'*[1]

THE ENERGY OF BELIEF

Believing in someone is an incredible gift you can give to their world. Knowing that someone believes in you can energize you and hands you the momentum needed to step out and take action. But at the end of the day, people are just people and I don't ever want to base my life on their level of belief. I never want to limit my destiny or live in the containment of what other people think I am capable of. Otherwise, what happens on the day someone says they don't believe in me? What happens on the day that they laugh at my dreams rather than applaud them? What happens when they throw water on the fire of my excitement rather than petrol?

I am so thankful to God for every person in my world who believes in me, they are my friends, my comrades, my partners in this journey of life. But I can never afford to substitute their belief in me for God's belief in me. Their belief on its own can never be enough. God designed it this way to deliver us from living lives that are constantly dependent on other people's approval.

The problem for many of us is that we equate how much God believes in us with how much our loved ones, pastor or friends believe in us, and the two are totally incomparable. Christ's belief in us can't be measured against anything because his belief in us is not shaken when our belief in him is. For many people, their belief in others comes with conditions. They clearly favour one over another and have more belief in the high achiever who they think is more gifted or capable. Their belief is determined by what they can see. You see it at school, in the work place, in families and sadly, it is prolific in churches.

We can end up convincing ourselves that God operates in the same way so we beat ourselves up by comparing our efforts to those around us. This then leads to a growing emergence of performance driven people and performance driven pastors who are working to gain people's approval. If you base your security in your popularity, then you are in trouble because there will be many times when you have to take decisions that people don't approve of, especially if you are in leadership.

You need to know that God is completely convinced about your potential, your ability and your future. His belief in you is guaranteed and it is belief in its purest form. He alone knows the extent of the inborn potential and ability that is in your life because he put it there. Yet even as I am writing these words, I know that many people who read them will struggle to accept that they are chosen, and that they have been appointed to bear fruit – fruit that will last.

PROVE THEM WRONG

I have experienced times when people have not believed in me and I am sure you will have too. Often it's not until you look back years later that you realise how key those situations were in your world. The decisions you make in the face of unbelief will shape you and your destiny.

As I have been writing this book and thinking about my own journey, I have recalled many instances when what people were saying about me and what God was saying were in conflict. When I was just fifteen years old I remember being at the home of a then leader in the church, who asked me what I wanted to do with my life. That night I opened my heart and shared how my ultimate dream was to work for my dad who was one of the pastors at the time. I told how I dreamed of helping him build and lead an awesome church. As I shared my dream I expected them to encourage me because I thought that wanting to serve God and help build his House was an awesome desire for any teenager to have. But they didn't encourage me, they didn't get excited with me and they certainly didn't believe in me. Their response that night was to laugh at first and then go on to explain all the reasons why it would never happen. They explained how I didn't have the right type of personality or gender to do that. They told me that family can't work with family, that I was too young, I lacked experience and that they didn't see a gift of leadership in me.

I could have let that experience crush me, but I couldn't let go of my dream. I had a choice to make. What did I believe more? Their opinion or what I knew God had whispered into my heart several years earlier. I went with God! Their lack of belief did not steal my dream but it did silence it for several years out of fear of others.

A few years later I was tested again. I took my A-levels and then went to university but couldn't find work after graduating. So, I applied for a job as a receptionist at a local double glazing firm. I went for the interview in a grotty showroom, with dirty seats and cigarette ash everywhere and sat there in my smart business suit thinking, 'What on earth am I doing here?' I knew without a doubt that this was definitely not what I wanted to do with my life, this was not my dream! But I had the interview and got a letter three days later. It read something like, 'Thank you for attending the interview. We are sorry to inform you that you are not qualified enough for a job with Northern Windows.'

Now that was a second blow to my confidence. I wasn't believed in by my leaders and now I wasn't even good enough for a double glazing firm! Again I had a choice to make, I could either park up on the fact that I had been rejected, or I could choose to believe that God still had his hand on my life and hadn't changed his mind about what he saw in me. So I tore up the letter, threw it in the bin and got the job section of the local paper out instead and moved on.

The reality is that right now you are actually reading the book of a Northern Windows reject! They didn't think I was qualified enough to run their office. They didn't think I had enough ability to give leadership to their filing cabinet! But God saw that I was qualified to help lead an awesome 21st century church. I often drive past that double glazing showroom because it is near my office. And when I pass it I smile and I thank God for the experience and for the lesson it taught me. Only your creator knows your inner worth and believing what he says about you is the only way to live.

It constantly amazes me, and is still hard for my brain to get around sometimes, that the Almighty God has chosen me and believes in me. I mean, I'm just Charlotte, I'm just a girl who lives in Bradford and yet God who created heaven and earth believes in me, and the same applies to you. Stop living your life at the level of your latest failed job interview, the failed relationship, your redundancy or your rejection letter from university, because none of these circumstances are a statement about your potential. These are temporary circumstances that you can learn and move on from.

GOD'S CHOICE

Throughout history God has taken people who no-one believed in and called them world changers.

Just look at David for instance. His own family didn't believe in him and he wasn't even invited to the party when Samuel went to anoint one of the brothers because they thought he wasn't important enough.[2] When you are secure like David, you don't mind not being invited to the anointing party. He was more than happy to stay on the hill and look after the sheep because his security was not in 'have I been included, does anyone notice I exist?' It was in God alone.

In their eyes he was just a kid, they didn't believe that he had it in him to be the next King of Israel. Even on the day he killed Goliath, David only went to the battle to take food for his brothers. He was in charge of the picnic and that day he carried cheese to the frontline to feed them. You've got to admit that being the cheese-carrier isn't the most glamorous of jobs to be doing on a battlefield. But David was happy to do any job because he only let what God said about him define him. Then that moment of opportunity came. All the men were in fear of Goliath, and David volunteered to fight him. But the response he got from all those close to him was one of total unbelief:

'When Eliab, David's oldest brother, heard him speaking with the men, he burned with anger at him and asked, "Why have you come down here? And with whom did you leave those few sheep in the desert? I know how conceited you are and how wicked your heart is; you came down only to watch the battle."' [3]

Eliab misread David's confidence that day and thought his brother was being conceited. But David's confidence was from his conviction that God's hand was on his life, and therefore David lived from his potential. He chose to ignore his family's unbelief. The truth is David showed up Eliab's unbelief and insecurity. He was furious with David for even suggesting he could fight Goliath because all he could see was his kid brother, who was only useful for looking after the sheep and making sandwiches. I mean, who did David think he was? That was the whole point, it wasn't about who Eliab thought he was, or about who the rest of his family thought he was, David stepped forward because he believed in who God said he was. He believed that God was with him so this big bully Goliath was no problem. God didn't see a shepherd boy, he didn't see a cheese-carrier, when God looked at David he saw a giant killer and he saw the future King of Israel.

Out of the thousands of men on the battlefield that day, David was probably one of the least qualified to take on Goliath. He was inexperienced, had never fought a man before, he wasn't used to wearing armour and didn't even have a sword of his own. It's the modern day equivalent of a top sports team pulling a supporter out of the stands and putting him on the pitch to play for them in the Cup Final because all the substitutes on the bench were too frightened. None of the others were willing to even try despite their military training, despite their armour, their swords and their vast experience on the battlefield. So what was their problem? I mean, this was the army of Israel we are talking about here; they served the same God as David. The issue was that they were unbelieving Believers, they just didn't believe enough to even have a go! They didn't believe God and therefore they didn't believe in themselves.

And what about Job? He was known for living a troubled life but his troubles didn't affect his belief. He also experienced the fickleness of people's belief and refused to let his faith be dragged down to their level. He went through so much suffering. He lost his health, possessions and his children were killed. And if that wasn't enough to go through, his closest friends who should have been there for him said it must be all his fault. They assumed Job must have sinned, that he must have done something really terrible for God to allow this to happen to him. His so called 'companions' laid the blame for his suffering firmly at Job's feet and urged him to repent. That's how much they believed in Job. Who needs friends like that when you're having a hard time? His own wife even told him to curse God and die! But if he had believed their words it would have caused him to question God, to question his goodness and love. Yet Job's reply to his wife in the midst of his trouble was a reaffirming of his belief in God and his refusal to let his circumstances second guess God's hand on his life. He said to her, '*You are talking like a foolish woman. Shall we accept good from God, and not trouble?*' [4]

Job discovered that other people's belief can never be enough, because when the circumstances were stacked against him not even his wife or his closest friends came through for him. Job was a believing Believer who had more confidence in God's Word and faithfulness than in what he could see with his human eyes. He believed in it more than the reality of his predicament and it was his deep belief in God that brought him through this time of extreme adversity. It gave him something the enemy can't touch - an unshakeable hope.

So how do you deal with people's lack of belief in you? You may not be ridiculed by your family like David was, and I hope you never go through as much suffering as Job, but their will be times in your life where you are put to the test. It is in trials like these that the faith of a believing Believer kicks in and an unbelieving Believer parks up. Some people do manage to pick themselves up eventually, but not until other people have affirmed them again. They need more people around to tell them how great they are doing, to stroke their ego again. But what if that doesn't happen? It didn't happen for David or for Job and you could spend your entire life waiting for it.

I have realised that I don't have to wait for someone else to call me, to make room for me or give me a pep talk to make me believe in myself. The source of my confidence and strength is God. If people say great things about you, that is just the icing on the cake, but make sure that you never let it become the cake!

God's total belief in you is a priceless gift that can never be taken away no matter what you face in life. His belief is assured, it doesn't change when you make a mistake or fail. If you use it properly it can be a powerful force in your life that will motivate and encourage you. God hasn't poured his belief into your world just to make you feel good about yourself. It is there for a reason and it is there for a purpose. You now need to 'do' something about it!

[1] John 15:15-16

[2] 1 Samuel 16

[3] 1 Samuel 17:28

[4] Job 2:9-10

Your belief can be revived, it can come back to life and the passion that first got you to believe can be re-ignited

Hezekiah's Prayer

14 ¶Then ᵇHezekiah took the ᶜletter from the hand of the messengers and read it, and he went up to the house of the LORD, and ᵈspread it out before the LORD.

15 Hezekiah prayed before the LORD and said, "O LORD, the God of Israel, ᵍwho are ʰenthroned above the cherubim, ⁱYou are the God, You alone, of all the kingdoms of the earth. You have made heaven and earth.

16 ʲIncline Your ear, O LORD, and hear; ᵏopen Your eyes, O LORD, and see; ...the words of Sennacherib, ...sent ...to reproach the living ...

13 'Where is the king of Hamath, the king of Arpad, the king of the city of Sep...
...arvaim, and of Hena and Ivvah?'

24 ...I dug wells and drank waters,
And with the sole of ...
...dried up
All the rivers of ²Egypt.'

25 ¶'Have you not heard?
Long ago I did it;
From ancient times I planned it to pass,
ⁿNow I have brought it to pass,
That you should turn fortified cities into ruinous heaps.

26 ᵒTherefore their inhabitants were short of strength,
They were dismayed and put to shame;
They were ᵖas the vegetation of the field and as the green herb,
As grass on the housetops is scorched before it is grown up.

27 ᵠBut ʳI know your sitting down,
And your going out and your coming in,
And ˢyour raging against Me.

Hezekiah's Illness a...
20 ¶In those days H...
ᵗmortally ill...
prophet the son of Am...
said to him, "Thus ...
your house in order ...
not live,"

2 Then he tu...
and prayed to the ...
3 ᵘ"Remember ...
seech You, in truth ...
You in truth ...
have done ...
And ᵛHez...

4 Be...
middle ...
to him ...

PAUL

DEC

When c...
JUST 2 b...
re may be other ...
bally tht u can't ...

ORN FOR SUCH A TIME ...THIS'

...metimes we don't ...wht
...ch a time as this'...

...THER IS a story abt CON...NCE
God working in the shadow...elying
people NOT in the shadows ...
...RAGEOUSLY.

...could dust ur life for GOD's FINGE...
...y are ALL OVER your life even ...
...t SEE / FEEL ...

believers are doers

'**S**how me your faith without deeds, and I will show you my faith by what I do. You believe that there is one God. Good! Even the demons believe that – and shudder.' [1]

This scripture requires us to stop and think about what it is saying; it needs to slap every believer in the face because it describes how God sees our belief in him. If you believe but there is no evidence of doing in your life, then as far as he is concerned your belief is on the same level as the demons! It is a wake up call to us all, especially to those who right now are coasting along in their Christianity, doing the bare minimum and thinking that somehow that is pleasing or helpful to God. I don't know about you, but I don't want it written about my life that I was a good person but sadly my believing was only equal to that of the demons!

DEAD OR ALIVE?

James goes on to say that 'faith without deeds is useless.'[2] So let's be honest here, if you have faith without deeds, just belief without doing, then that belief is as good as dead. For many Christians 'dead' is a good word to describe how their walk with God feels. Their faith is lifeless, their Christianity is bland, dull and boring; it has simply died. It is the equivalent of having a car with no petrol in the tank. You have the right vehicle to get you to your destination but you are missing a vital element and you are certainly not going to get anywhere in a hurry. Every move you make takes extreme effort as you try to jump start your faith by pushing it along the road.

The only way to get your engine started and get you moving again is to fill your tank up with the fuel of a living faith. That will get you re-enthused, re-motivated and re-energized. If you have ever broken down you will know that sitting in your car at the side of the road while everyone else zooms past is not a great way to spend your time. It is frustrating, embarrassing and often leads to hours of boredom while you wait for someone to help you get going again. You sit there motionless and have to watch as everyone else overtakes you. For many this is how they feel about their Christianity. Their life seems to be happening in slow motion and their lack of faith causes them to be frightened and intimidated by the speed of the passing traffic. Getting back on the road seems just too daunting so they decide to stay in the safety of the lay-by.

Sitting at the side of the road reduces you to being a spectator in life and Believers who have settled for this find that their faith quickly runs dry. They soon become disillusioned as their walk with God grinds to a stand still, because they are not going anywhere or doing anything for him. Doing is your spiritual ignition key and without it you will never manage to restart your engine and continue your journey. Believers who have stopped doing, find that their passion for God begins to fade away. Instead, they find their main source of fulfillment and excitement in hobbies, activities and other interests rather than in their faith. Reading the Bible, praying and their experience of church becomes more of a duty they perform than something they look forward to. Church becomes somewhere they catch up with their list of things to do or on the latest gossip. If the prayer meeting is just where you catch up with your friends or on your sleep, then something is wrong! It's time to stop spectating and get back on the road.

HAS BOREDOM SET IN?

Jesus came to give you life in abundance, [3] and an abundant life is definitely the opposite of a bored life. So, how do we remedy spiritual boredom, how do you get that spark back into your spiritual walk? The good news is that your belief can be revived, it can come back to life and the passion that first got you to believe can be re-ignited.

To help you understand how, think about your relationship with God as if it was a marriage partnership. If your marriage was in crisis, if you were bored with your partner then as a couple you would do something about it. You would seek to put things right and you would review where it went wrong. You'd be left with the following options:

Option 1: You settle for a mundane married life and live with an 'it'll do but nothing much ever happens here' type of relationship. And for many, that describes where they have let their relationship with God get to.

Option 2: You separate and leave the marriage. In our scenario this means you quit your faith, backslide and go looking for excitement elsewhere. The prodigal tried this and it doesn't work.

Option 3: You 'do' something about it. This requires you to put in some hard work which is why it is often the least popular choice. It demands that you roll up your sleeves and get busy. It means you have to take your life off autopilot, get hold of the controls and put yourself back on course with your destiny to alleviate the boredom that has set into your walk with God. It is the only option that will work!

If your faith is dead then don't just sit there expecting God to resuscitate you. If you are bored with church and your level of Christianity then stop waiting for your pastor to give you the 'electric shock' treatment every Sunday morning through his sermon! The truth is, if there is a problem in your relationship with God then it is from your end. How can a relationship with the creator of the universe ever be dull? How can your belief in the one who gave life, be lifeless?

To banish the boredom and revive your faith, you need to ask yourself some questions. What are you currently doing for God that scares you? What are you currently trying that stretches you? Where are you serving that challenges you? What are you asking for in your prayer life that demands something from you and not just from God? You need to start taking action.

DOING IS THE CURE

Today, if you find your faith is dead or if your spiritual pulse is weak, then don't worry. Doing can bring it back to life; it can give you a living, breathing faith once again. Let me show you what I mean by looking at a verse that as Christians we all say we believe. You have probably got it highlighted in your

Bible and will have no doubt heard it preached from many times over. But like all the promises in God's Word it can be either dead or alive in your life, and the person who determines that is you!

'The spirit of the Sovereign Lord is on me, because the Lord has anointed me to preach good news to the poor. He has sent me to bind up the broken hearted, to proclaim freedom for the captives.'[4]

For many Believers what we just read is simply information, a suggestion but not a reality. But your faith in these words only really lives when you act upon them. Don't you want to know what it feels like to be the person who tells the poor in spirit that they can live a rich life? Don't you want to experience the heart felt gratitude that comes from the brokenhearted when you take the time to stop and bind up their wounds? Don't you want to put your arms around the grieving and comfort them in their time of mourning?

Doing what you say you believe will transform your life and the lives of others. In our church we have over one hundred and seventy ministries because we have encouraged people to read God's Word and then empowered them to go and do it. So they start a ministry to the poor, they reach the hurting, they visit the sick, they befriend the lonely and they feed the hungry. They don't have a lifeless faith but a life giving faith.

BELIEVING ENERGISES DOING

Now, I have noticed that many Christians actually talk a lot about 'doing'. Many churches and leaders can have a tendency to try and pressure people through their preaching and appeals to do more, serve more and give more. But this is an exhausting and depressing way to lead. It's like putting the cart before the horse. You spend all your time trying to push when God has given you the facility to pull. Believing is the horse which allows you to pull all the things you want to do into being.

It really is effortless when the two are working together, you don't have to force anything. When we launched a campaign for people to give to the building of our new Champions Centre here at the Abundant Life Church, we saw this in motion. By the end of the first day when the vision had been shared with just a few of our team and leaders the money was already beginning to pour in. The official giving date was still more than two months away, so we could allow people time to understand what they were giving to. Yet we found that the belief level of many in our church was so deeply rooted in our leadership and our vision that they didn't need convincing to do anything. This was expressed through their amazing response. A spontaneous willingness to 'do', that is not forced and is not coerced or brought about by the persuasion of leaders is, I believe, one of the signs of a healthy church.

People don't resist doing more when it springs from a passionate belief. So as leaders we need to aim to ensure that what we believe and what we are imparting is not merely head knowledge. I can honestly say that what we believe about reaching our city, helping the needy and influencing our community is so embedded in the heart of our church, that we never have a problem finding doers. When a person truly believes in something they will commit to it, give to it, serve it and involve in it. It's a fact of life, just look at political campaigners, world leaders, society changers and human rights activists. It's their belief that inspires them to keep going and therefore their doing is shaping your world and mine whether you agree with them or not! The church needs to wake up for we should be the biggest shapers of the world we live in. We should believe more in God's Word than any politician believes in their manifesto.

So if you want to stretch your doing you need to work on your believing first. God's relying on you and me to believe more so that we will do more.

A PHOTOGRAPHIC FAITH

So, what 'doing' is accompanying your believing? If you say you believe you can be sure that God will be looking for a corresponding action to see whether you mean it or not.

For me, starting the Cherish women's conference was one

of those believing and doing challenges. I knew it was a God idea, but there is a big difference between believing that and putting a date in the diary, booking speakers and wondering whether anyone would turn up! It was a risk but one worth taking because today Cherish is blessing the lives of thousands of women from across the world. But I could have kept my believing on the shelf and never done anything about it. I think far too many God opportunities have been wasted because believers didn't convert to being doers.

If you have faith you should always be able to show something for it. It will be far more than words, it will have an outworking and it will make memories that you can look back over throughout your life time.

I have a photograph album of what my faith looks like, I have a picture of the very first day I preached at church which shows my believing and doing working together. If I hadn't done it, I could still be sat in church today saying, 'I think God wants to use me to speak,' but doing nothing about it while the years rolled by.

Some of my pictures are real photographs but others are moments that I have captured and stored away in my mind to remind me of those times when I did something special. Like the first time I brought a friend to church, and when I shared my testimony at school. I remember praying for my neighbour, writing my first book, and the list goes on.

You need to have similar snapshots of your own life. Do you have a picture in your mind of when you first reached out to people in your community, first led someone to Christ or blessed someone with an act of kindness? You need to mark these occasions because they represent the coming together of your faith and deeds.

THE COMPLETION TEST

God loves genuine faith, he loves it when people trust him completely and he will test you in this because he needs to know if you are the real deal. He will bring situations into your world that have the potential to bridge the gap between your believing and doing. It's what I call the completion test.

Abraham sat one of these tests at a crucial stage in his life when God asked him to sacrifice Isaac. James wrote: '*Was not our ancestor Abraham considered righteous for what he did when he offered his son Isaac on the altar? You see that his faith and his actions were working together, and his faith was made complete by what he did.*' [5]

Can you imagine how he must have felt that day? His belief was certainly being tested to the limit. Isaac was his only child and now he was being asked to sacrifice him. It made no sense and when Abraham lifted the knife above Isaac to kill him, he didn't know it was just a test but he was still willing to go through with it. Abraham believed in God's faithfulness and plan for his life more than what he was feeling. His belief was stronger than his emotional attachment to his son, he was more convinced about God's plan for Isaac's life than his own plan for his son's life. Until you come to these moments you don't know how rich, you don't know how real, and you don't know how deep your belief is. Abraham's believing and doing were walking hand in hand that day. His faith in that moment was made complete by his obedience to follow through. It is these tests that demand something from you, they are an opportunity to make your life stand out from the crowd and demonstrate the genuineness of your belief.

Abraham was considered righteous because of what he did, not because he talked about it. When his belief was tested he did exactly what God had told him and put his son on the altar. He was saying 'my belief in God is stronger than my belief in myself.' Abraham passed the test with flying colours that day and sometimes God just wants to see whether you are serious about doing what he has asked or not. These completion tests come at significant stages in your journey and passing them qualifies you to move on to the next level of life, leadership and responsibility.

'Isaac' moments are scary, they are defining and they are precious. They are certainly not boring and they bring your belief to life. So please don't avoid them, embrace them, let them provoke you and bring you to a place of completion. Abraham's faith was '*made complete by what he did*' and the same is true of your faith and mine.

[1] James 2:18-19

[2] James 2:20

[3] John 10:10

[4] Isaiah 61:1

[5] James 2:21-22

You need a photograph album of what your faith looks like memories you can look back on and enjoy.

CHAPTER 4

first followers

The guy who invented bungee jumping must have believed he had a great idea because he had to go first! He entrusted his life and entire world to a piece of elastic at the end of his ankle! But he so believed in his invention and that piece of elastic, that he was willing to fling his body into oblivion believing he would live! He had more belief in elastic than many people have in God!

That person who did the first bungee jump made a way for all the people after him to share that experience. Today it's a popular adventure sport that millions have now experienced. They jump with the proven knowledge that they can survive and spiritually, our walk with God is exactly the same. We can either be the ones who jump after it's proven to be safe or we can be like the one who took the risk first. A crowd may have followed but one person went first!

God is looking for people like that, he desperately needs men and women who are willing to go first, to take what they believe and try to achieve it so others can follow. This type of person is what I have called a 'first follower'.

A first follower acts first and thinks later. They have the courage to launch the initiative, speak up and step out. They write the book, do the ministry and go out and raise the funds. They get on with whatever God has given them to do without delay and have the guts to do it before everyone else.

First followers are the first to give and they have already sown their money while others are still looking around to see what everyone else is doing. They are the first to sign up to help in a ministry area, they don't wait to find out what their friends are doing and involve because of peer pressure. First followers let God interrupt their world at any time. He has first priority in their busy lives. The Holy Spirit is their alarm clock and as soon as they hear it ring, they stop what they are doing and follow his prompting. No sooner has the alarm gone off and they are out there making things happen, while others around them are rubbing the sleep out of their eyes and telling them to calm down and take it easy. But when you are a first follower you can't calm down! You just know that God is prompting you and asking you to do something, so you simply step out and try it.

This actually starts to simplify your life because it cuts out all the questions and second guessing of what God wants to do.

It removes from your life all the hours spent talking about your options and going over them again and again with various people groups, all the while delaying you from getting anything done. First followers break through containments and dismantle potential speed bumps in their world. You just believe that heaven is behind you and believe that God is telling you to go. You will never see the sign, 'Do not disturb' on the door of a first follower's life. Instead, they make a point of asking, 'God please do disturb me, I am highly interruptible'.

Too many Christians are so inflexible in what they will and won't do for God. They have set up strict limits on what they will involve in and how much time they will commit. They have made certain areas of their life 'no go zones' to the Holy Spirit. As far as they are concerned, if God is going to use their lives he will have to do things on their terms and in their timing. I am sure you don't need me to tell you that God doesn't take orders, he gives them.

Being a first follower is not to do with gifting or ability, it is to do with obedience and availability. It is a choice that you have the power to make. It means deciding to try something different and to be willing to risk failing rather than to keep playing it safe. It's living outside the permissions of other people and, because of this first followers are often seen as being single-minded, forceful and impatient. All they can see is what God wants to happen and they feel an urgency in their spirit to get on with it, even if that means being misunderstood.

SECOND HAND FAITH

It's always special to share with someone a 'first'. There is a unique joy as you see someone try to do something they have never done before. I became really aware of this in the first years of Hope's life. We were right there with her as she did things for the first time. We were there when she had her first chocolate ice-cream on her own and believe me that was worth seeing. She had ice-cream everywhere, in her hair, round her face, and on her clothes. In fact she ended up wearing more than she ate but we loved watching the joy it brought her. She will do it better each time, and hopefully get less messy in her approach! But the first time experience is always special. For Hope, the first time will always be the one where she got to make the most mess and therefore had the most fun!

I am convinced we are supposed to have first experiences throughout our entire lifetime, not just during our childhood. We should always be learning more and trying new things. Too many people leave those first experiences behind them once they enter adulthood and trade them in for a lifestyle of second hand living. They live life cautiously, always holding back and refusing to take any risks.

When you live your life with this second hand mentality, you settle for listening to other people recall their stories of adventures that you didn't have the courage to embark upon. It's like having someone describe their luxurious holiday to you. They can tell you the colour of the water, the heat of the sun, the smell of the sea breeze, the music in the background and the perfect sunsets. They can show you the pictures and even play you the video, but you and I both know that it isn't the same as seeing it for yourself. I'm not happy until I've been and put my own toes in the sand, seen the sunset with my own eyes and swam in the ocean myself. I don't ever want to make do with second hand experiences in my Christianity. God never intended that for any of us. That would be settling for less than his best for our lives as he has so many 'firsts' that he wants us all to enjoy.

If you don't ever try anything first you are reducing your life to painting by numbers. You are just waiting for others to tell you what colours to use and where. That is such an unremarkable way to live when God has given you a blank canvas and placed a whole array of colours inside your life which need to be expressed. They are unique, vibrant and perfectly matched to the destiny he has planned for your life. You can choose to sit and stare at that blank canvas for the rest of your life and admire everyone else's artwork, or you can draw on what God has put inside your life and turn what was an ordinary looking canvas into an extraordinary masterpiece. The choice is yours.

First followers in action

If you are willing to go first, history will record the amazing things you will do and achieve during your lifetime.

Think about Moses who, at the grand old age of eighty,

approached the King of Egypt and told him to let his entire workforce go. He demanded that he set all the Israelite slaves free, with no warning and without even offering suitable replacements. He must have really believed that he was hearing God because he was risking his own life by saying something so radical. After those encounters, Moses walked out of Egypt first. It was worth it for the sake of the people and three million captives who followed him to freedom, thanking God for the courage of that first follower.

Just look at the life of Noah, he was the first ever boat builder. In fact, he was so far ahead of everyone else that they thought he was crazy - a common misconception held about most first followers but you get used to it eventually! Imagine trying to build a massive boat in a land that had never seen rain and then putting two of every animal on the earth in it. He must have been a source of entertainment in that neighbourhood for many years. I am sure everyone was laughing at him behind his back, until the first drop of rain fell! Building the ark was a big project, there was plenty of time for Noah to get cold feet about the idea and give up. I am sure there were a lot of times when he sat down and thought, 'What if this goes wrong? But God, what if there is no flood, and what if the animals fight? And what if my wife doesn't like the idea of living in a floating zoo, she is not all that keen on animals you know!'

Many Christians live permanently in the land of 'what if'. It stops them from trying anything because every time they have an idea that is a bit different or daring they sit and think about what could go wrong. This kind of talk won't get you anywhere because God is not interested in your 'what ifs!' He is interested in your 'Yes', and your, 'I'll do it' and your, 'I believe you'. If you are living with a 'what if' mentality, you need to start focusing on what could go right with what God has put in your heart. Ask yourself, 'what if God blessed it, what if God used it, what if God's hand was on it?'

I certainly don't want to die and have the words 'What if' written on my tombstone. 'What if she had lived to her true potential? What if she had used that ability. What if she had dared to do everything God had asked; she could have led an amazing life.' I want God to be able to give me first follower plans, first follower ideas and I want to always have first follower faith. I have chosen to live like that and so can you. God has the same belief in you right now that he had in Noah. The question is, do you believe enough to go first?

I am sure that Noah was faced with plenty of unbelief from those around him. I am sure there must have been times when even his own family had some serious discussions about whether he had gone completely mad. But he kept on going, he kept on hammering those nails in day after day and building that ark no matter what anyone else thought about him, because he trusted in what God had said. No-one in Noah's town had ever seen a boat before, he created a completely new method of transport, he opened up new possibilities, he came up with an alternative that had not been thought of before, one that others could follow.

PIONEERING NEW PATHS

Have you ever reached the end of the official footpath out in the countryside and noticed a new path that had been started? One day someone walked to the end of the tarmac and decided their journey was not yet over. They wanted to travel further, they wanted to explore, so they left the established path and made their own way.

It amazes me that what they unintentionally started as they walked that day became the path that everyone else then followed. Hundreds of pairs of feet since theirs have walked in their footsteps and worn the path down, but why? Was that the only option? Surely other paths would have been just as direct and surely other people could have decided to walk in a different direction! The real reason for this is that most people would rather follow someone else's lead even if they are not sure where it's taking them. They believe it is safer sticking with what has already been tried and tested.

First followers are the type of people who aren't content to make do with what has been done before. Their faith is pace-setting, it takes the lead and goes off the beaten track. It leaves the well worn footpaths that have already been taken by so many others and sets off to find new ways and discover new exciting destinations. First followers challenge old ways of thinking, they break away from tradition and 'status quo behaviour' to do something fresh. They can be found in every walk of life, they are the entrepreneurs, they are the people on the cutting edge of business, they are the people who start new initiatives and achieve what other people said could not be done. They are trailblazers who pioneer new routes for other people to walk on, and that is why we need them in the House of God. We need church leaders who are not frightened to cut new paths in their communities and in their leadership styles, to establish new roads that others can follow. If we don't do this then we reduce our churches and our communities to following others, and resign ourselves to making do with what has been done before. We live with second hand belief.

When our Senior Pastor Paul Scanlon set out to build the relevant 21st century church we are today, he forged a new pathway. The journey we took is explained in his book, 'Crossing Over'. He is a first follower who refused to be content to travel on the well established road of having a mediocre church that wasn't reaching people and wasn't impacting and helping our community. The route he took was new to everyone, we were never sure what was around the next bend in the road, but we knew that we just had to keep on following God's voice that was calling us to go further.

Being a first follower takes you off the map and into uncharted territory and this can be a hair-raising experience at times. You can't ask anyone for directions because no-one has been there before, but your inner compass, the Holy Spirit, keeps you on course.

The path we made when we 'crossed over' is now being followed by other people. Other churches have been inspired by our journey because they got a glimpse of the destination it would take them to. The route is now becoming established as extra pairs of feet travelling on it wear it down and leave a trail for those who will follow in the future. We have been able to draw them a map, we can let them know what to expect on the way, and warn them about the pitfalls they may face. That is what happens when you are a first follower. You don't just take yourself on a journey, you will bring people with you; they will follow in your footsteps.

Living as a first follower is exciting, but it means that sometimes you have to go it alone while everyone else holds back and waits to see what happens to you! Going first does mean you have to take risks, but if God has told you to do it, is it really a risk? It may feel like one but he isn't trying to set you up, everything he will ever ask you to do is totally possible, it is completely achievable.

I am not for a moment suggesting that first followers have absolutely no qualms about what they do. They are not a breed of Christian superheroes, many of them do it scared and with their knees knocking. Their conviction about who God is and what he has called them to do keeps them focused on their assignment. It is this that makes their belief far stronger than their doubt.

CHAPTER 5

can't or won't?

Doubt and belief are like oil and water - they just don't mix and if you want to be someone who responds to God's voice and does amazing things then you will have to deal with this issue in your life. Doubt whispers to you, it tells you that you can't make it, that you can't achieve it, that you can't do it and starts to build-up a layer of unbelief in your mind. This layered living will not get you very far because every time you are about to step out, the oil of doubt will float to the top of your life and smother your belief.

Doubt is not a new problem, in fact it was what separated man from God in the garden of Eden and has been with us ever since. It says, 'Now the serpent ... said to the woman, "Did God really say, 'You must not eat from any tree in the garden'?"'

¹That innocent sounding question, 'Did God really say?' was a turning point for Eve and the rest of humanity. Doubt entered her heart subtly and deceitfully. The thing about doubt is, it's not always easy to spot, it doesn't present itself to you with warning signs saying, 'Doubt warning, if you let this enter your heart it could derail your destiny!' It is a far more undetectable tool of the enemy, one that can manoeuvre you in the wrong direction and have you heading towards unbelief before you even realise it. When the serpent approached Eve, he didn't say 'Today I am going to lead you into disobedience!' Doubt entered with a simple suggestion.

How many times have you questioned something God has told you? Have you ever questioned his love for you, his faithfulness, his forgiveness, and have you ever questioned his purpose for your life? I mean, what harm can there be in asking a question, it doesn't even feel like you are sinning and that is why we need to be so careful.

SLOW PUNCTURES

Doubt of any size is like a small puncture in the tyre of your life. It slowly undermines your belief, it questions, it nags, it challenges you and says, 'Who do you think you are? You can't do this. This is impossible, go back! You are a failure!' Doubt shouts to you in an attempt to cut short that which belief has birthed.

A lot of people don't realise doubt has taken up residency in their lives. It can appear in different forms and often it shows up as 'belief' but of the wrong kind. I've heard people say, 'You get what you expect' many times and this is so true. Your belief is not neutral; it is either positive or negative and sets the coordinates of where you will end up. Doubt twists belief around and produces negative faith in the lives of Believers which works against them instead of for them.

You may have experienced this if you have you ever attempted something that in all honesty, you didn't believe you could do. I can remember taking my first driving test. It makes me shudder just to think about it. I was so convinced I would fail, that the truth was I had failed before I even got in the car. It was a complete waste of money because I believed the driving instructor didn't like me, I believed he was having a bad day and therefore he was going to fail me. So it was no surprise when he did. My unbelief in myself, my ability, and the driving instructor made for a very tense, stressful and painful hour in the car. But I determined it, no one else. That day my power of belief was working in the wrong direction and we can be like that with God. Our lack of belief in his promises and our unbelief in what we are capable of makes for an uncomfortable journey of our own choosing.

Doubt is something that every believer has to face. Whenever God asks you to do something the enemy will try to sow seeds of doubt in your mind and your heart to stop you in your tracks. At times like these many people refuse to move another inch, they say 'I can't do this, I can't go any further!' But let's be honest, most people who say 'I can't' actually mean 'I won't' and those two words are a world apart. Doubt knocks your reasoning off track and instead of getting on with the job in hand, people reel off a list of poor excuses that are just not going to impress anyone, especially God.

The 'I can't' versus 'I won't' contest is where many Believers get stuck. Every time you say, 'I can't', stop yourself and think about whether that is the truth. Is it really about your ability? Are you really unable to do what God has asked of you or are you unwilling, or maybe just scared? It's not a new problem, even the disciples struggled with this although they were close to Jesus and did life with him 24/7. One such occasion was when they were caught in the middle of a storm on Lake Galilee. Let's take a closer look at what happened that day.

Imagine what it must have been like for them. It was the middle of the night and they were a long way from the shore. The boat was being tossed around by the wind and the waves. And if that wasn't enough to contend with, they saw a ghostly figure making its way across the water towards them. This was not the pleasant boat trip they had hoped for when they set off with the rest of the disciples earlier that day. They were cold, wet, frightened out of their wits and wanted to know where on earth Jesus was when they needed him!

But then they heard a voice, it was familiar to them, it was Jesus and he was saying 'Come!' So what would you do? Would you be itching to give it a go and step out or would getting out of the boat be last on your list of smart moves? That was the decision facing the disciples that day out on Lake Galilee. They all saw the same, they all heard the same words, but only Peter said 'I can'. [2]

'I CAN' BREEDS POSSIBILITIES

You will never know what you are capable of; you will never know what you can do until you say 'I can' and start living your belief out alongside God's amazing power. Peter didn't know he could walk on water until he tried and if he had refused to get out of the boat that day he would never have discovered his unusual talent. There are some things in life that you know you can do but there are far more things you could do. The only reason you haven't discovered them is because you haven't tried.

Our daughter Hope Cherish learned to walk as part of her physical development. We didn't need to push her into it, or enrol her for walking lessons, it just came naturally to her, but she doesn't instinctively know how to drive a car. I am sure that one day she will learn that skill, but if she never has the courage to get behind the wheel she will never find out she can do it.

In the same way we need to be willing to at least try, otherwise we will live a contained, boat bound existence. Every one of the disciples could have walked on water that day because Jesus wasn't being exclusive and favouring Peter above the others. It was actually Peter himself who recognised the voice of Jesus and said, 'Lord if it's you, tell me to come'. He made walking on water an option for his life, he was saying 'Jesus, I can do this and I want to be where you are. Here I come!'

CLOSING THE GAP

Maybe right now you are saying 'I can't' to something God has asked you to do because you have more belief in your ability to sink than in your ability to walk on water. You have more belief in the power of the wind and the waves you can see than in the power of God. Yes, you believe in Jesus but you believe more in gravity. This isn't a valid excuse for staying in the boat when God is calling you. I think that sometimes saying 'I can't' can make us feel justified about being disobedient, we go for the sympathy vote. The reality is we don't need sympathy, we need courage.

You need to know that God has called you, empowered you, and believes in you, but he won't get out of the boat for you. That is your part. So if you are waiting for God to do everything for you, it is going to be a long wait. He is watching you and cheering you on because he knows how much you will benefit from doing it yourself. That is why there are some gaps in life that God won't close. There are some distances he won't go for you because in that gap is an experience which will change your life. If he was to remove the gap it would mean that you would bypass your opportunity to learn and grow. There is simply no substitute for that.

So be warned all God's 'little helpers' out there who are trying to close gaps for others. You are actually making it harder and are stunting other people's growth. I have met a lot of underdeveloped Christians who are spiritually underweight, they are lacking maturity and depth and are missing the richness and wisdom these gaps will hand them. If we are not careful we will create a generation of Believers who have never put anything to the test. It is the equivalent of handing out life jackets to keep people afloat. We keep their heads above water and prevent them from drowning but in the process take away their need to ever learn to swim. They are going to miss out on the experience of a lifetime because we thought we were being helpful!

Sometimes leaders can be overprotective and controlling,

spending much of their time building bridges rather than trusting individuals to find their own way to the other side. This can cause people to have an unhealthy reliance on their leaders to do everything for them. I have had to learn that there is more than one way to do things and my job is to guide and lead, but not to replace people's belief in God with a belief that I will keep rescuing them. It's our job to be the swimming coaches, shouting words of encouragement and teaching people how to improve their stroke, not the lifeguards who stand there policing the pool, telling people to be careful when they jump in at the deep end or somersault off the diving board. Our tendency should be to push people in rather than to pull them out. We need to be willing to let people sink in order to discover what is inside them. It is the only way they will realise what they can do.

TAKING THE PLUNGE

I certainly thank God for every 'out of the boat' experience I have had. I am also grateful to the people who have stood next to me saying, 'it's your turn to take the plunge!'

I remember sitting in my dad's office one day sharing something God had put on my heart that had really inspired me. I suggested that maybe it would be something good for him to say to the church. He responded enthusiastically saying, 'That sounds great but God didn't give it to me to say, he gave it to you – what is wrong with your mouth? Are you free to speak next Sunday?'

He refused to close the gap for me that day and left me with an in or out of the boat choice. When he asked me to speak it was my equivalent of Jesus saying 'Come' to Peter and I had to decide what to do. That week I took my first Sunday Service and preached to our church. I would love to say I did it with stature, charisma and confidence, but the truth is I was physically sick four times before the meeting and then I spoke too fast, thinking that the faster I spoke the quicker it would be over. But I walked on water and that day I closed a gap in my life by walking the distance and that first step is now many years behind me. Now I speak with confidence, I don't get so nervous that I feel ill before I get up. But if it wasn't for that experience, I wouldn't be ready for the other things God is now asking me to do.

THAT SINKING FEELING

The truth is, every time you step out you might find yourself sinking, it's a risk you have to take. Maybe you are reading this and you are exactly in that position. You took a couple of steps on the water but now you are going under. You believed enough to step out and try but that belief did not bank on the storm and the gale force wind coming, and now you are under pressure.

If you are someone who has a sinking feeling right now, I celebrate you. Your believing got you somewhere, it got you on the water and you trusted God enough to step into the unknown. Even though you're sinking, don't lose heart because you are in good company, Peter sank and I have on many occasions. So let's look at the reasons why we can find ourselves going under.

CONSISTENCY

'Then Peter got down out of the boat, walked on the water and came toward Jesus. But when he saw the wind, he was afraid and, beginning to sink, cried out "Lord save me!" Immediately Jesus reached out his hand and caught him. "You of little faith," he said, "why did you doubt?"' [3]

Peter's experience of walking on water was short lived. It lasted only for as long as his belief held out. Yes, he doubted, he took his eyes off Jesus and looked at the wind and the waves, but he was also lacking something that is essential if you are ever going to walk more than a few steps - consistency!

Consistency is what will keep you afloat. Inconsistent people ebb and flow in their emotions, in their attitudes and their belief in God. One day they want to be the first out of the boat and the next they don't even want to get in it to sail across the lake! Too many people start well but give up mid journey. They commit to serve then pull out when the demand on them gets too much. They pledge their support until it becomes unpopular. They fail to follow through because of their inconsistency.

Lasagne Sheets

A while ago some friends of ours were coming for dinner so I decided to make something quick and easy, a lasagne. Now, I can make a great lasagne, but on this day as everyone sat around the table and I tried to cut into the lasagne, the whole dish collapsed in on itself. I was so embarrassed and apologised profusely for my awful cooking as I served up the runny lasagne with a soup ladle! All the time I was wondering what had gone wrong. I had made lasagne plenty of times and this had never happened before. I went to bed still thinking about it and suddenly woke up in the middle of the night with my answer. I hadn't put any pasta in it! I had put plenty of layers of mince, then cheese sauce but had forgotten to put the lasagne sheets in between. It was the wrong consistency because there was a vital ingredient missing.

The lasagne sheets would have made that dish the right consistency. They would have held the layers together and that is exactly how belief works in your life. You can keep adding layers to your life by doing more for God but without belief underpinning it, the consistency will be all wrong. What you are doing won't be solid and it won't be stable.

Wherever you are at right now, in the boat, out of the boat or walking on water, you need to know that God is saying the same to you as he said to Peter. He is saying 'come' and he has every right to do that – because he knows you can do it. He's not teasing you, it is because he believes in you. He knows that you are capable of going beyond what you have done before.

So, what will your response be? 'I can,' 'I can't', or 'I won't?' If like Peter you always say 'I can', you may still get wet, there will be times when you get that sinking feeling but the wind and the waves aren't enough to stop you trying. No-one remembers Peter as being the disciple who sank, they remember him for walking on water, for those few steps he took. What do you want to be remembered for?

[1] Genesis 3:1-3
[2] Matthew 14:22-23
[3] Matthew 14:29-31

Sometimes we need to let people sink... in order to discover what's inside them.

This belongs to
Sonia Freeman

THIS BOOK
BELONGS TO
MATT

YOU NEED TO UNDERSTAND
THAT GOD HAS EXPECTATIONS
ON YOUR LIFE BECAUSE
YOU HAVE SOMETHING
THAT BELONGS TO HIM.

CHAPTER 6

much entrusted

When you got saved your life took on an eternal purpose and now there are many people that God wants to touch, bless and reach through you. He doesn't want you to keep his truth or his belief in you to yourself. He doesn't want you to be spiritually overweight while people in your community, church and world are hungry and crying out for just one bite of what you have! All your believing and doing is not just so you can have an exciting, fulfilled Christian life, it is for you to use to help other people.

Some Christians have just enough belief to get by in their own world but believing they are gifted enough to influence and bless other people, is a step too far. Yet the reality is that God believes in you because you have so much to give!

It doesn't belong to you

'From everyone who has been given much, much will be demanded; and from the one who has been entrusted with much, much more will be asked.' [1] This scripture says that 'much has been entrusted' to us. So, whether we think this is true or not, we are all sitting on a deposit from God. An entrustment is something you look after for someone else, it is on loan; it doesn't actually belong to you.

If someone loans you their car, you look after it in a different way to the way you would if they actually gave it to you. Although you can use it and enjoy it, you drive it carefully because you know they are coming back for it. So, any dints or scratches you put in the side of it are repaired quickly and if you spill anything on the interior, you get it cleaned up. They have entrusted it to your care and they have a certain expectation of the condition their car will be in when you return it to them. But if they had given it to you, they have no right to complain or ask what you did with their old car once the keys were in your possession.

You need to understand that God has expectations about your life because you have got something that belongs to him. He has deposited things in your world which you are supposed to be looking after. The ownership of all you have is heaven sent but it is for earthly use. It says in 2 Timothy, *'Guard the good deposit that was entrusted to you.'* [2] We are all guardians of our entrustment and God is holding you and I accountable for the investment he has made in us.

PORTION CONTROL

When God made you, he created you for a purpose and he chose what he would invest in your life. He didn't just throw out gifts randomly to his children. His distribution of gifts was perfectly and forensically arranged. Like any good investor, he weighed up the potential return on your life first. Don't get the wrong idea here, God is not showing favouritism or making one person more important than another, he just knows what you are capable of handling. He knows the right amount to pack into your world and what you can carry without making your load too heavy.

I will never forget returning from an overseas trip some years ago and ending up behind a flustered couple in the airline check-in queue. They were returning home from their vacation and had obviously done all their Christmas, birthday and anniversary shopping for the next ten years! They must have bought for every relative in their extended family and a few others besides. As they hauled their luggage onto the check in scales they were told the bad news; they were seriously over the baggage weight restriction. They had a choice to make, either pay for the excess baggage or lose it. So they hauled their bags to the side of the check in queue and began the embarrassing process of emptying their contents in front of the whole line of now very impatient travellers. The stuff in those cases was beyond belief! I then watched in amazement as their strategy to outsmart the ticket lady from charging them an excess baggage fee unfolded. They started to put on layers of clothing to lighten their load. At the end of this entertaining process they were wearing seventeen items of extra clothing each. They looked more like sumo wrestlers than the couple who had tried to check in earlier!

That picture has stuck with me as a reminder of how in life we need to know the load we were built to carry and stick to it. We don't need to go through the embarrassment of trying to put on things that we were never supposed to wear. We don't need the embarrassment of being told we are overweight and neither do we want to be found with lots of empty space we could have filled. That is why God handed out to us the right portion and weight restriction for our lives. It says in Matthew that his *'yoke is easy and his burden is light'*.[3] Why? Because it is tailor made to be the perfect amount of weight that you were created to carry.

So what is your weight limit, what can you handle? The answer is evident when you look at what God has placed in your life. Your weight restriction has already been set and will be different from the person next to you. You may be able to carry more or less than them but you don't determine that. Therefore you don't need to concern yourself with what you have or haven't got, your job is simply to know what size of portion you can handle.

This was explained by Jesus in the parable of the talents.[4] It was about a master who gave one, two and five talents respectively to three of his servants, each according to their ability. Sometime later he returned to find out what they had done with his money. Two of the servants had used it wisely and gained more, but the servant who only had one talent hid it in the ground and did nothing.

God's expectations for your life are in proportion to what he has given you. So you can't sit there thinking, 'I'm OK because I have used two of my talents,' when he gave you three. You will need to account for that third one and explain why you did nothing with it. The master was absolutely furious with the servant who did nothing with his talent and said, '*throw that worthless servant outside into the darkness where there will be weeping and gnashing of teeth*'.[5] I certainly don't want God to feel that way about my life because I wasted his valuable investment in me.

STOP DAWDLING

Three servants were given the same opportunity, yet two of them were successful and one failed miserably. I have often wondered why only two of them made the most of it. The difference was in their response to the demand placed on them. We read that '*The man who had received the five talents went at once and put his money to work and gained five more.*'[6] To be a 'five talent servant' you need to have an 'at once' attitude. These two small words, 'at once', are why some people increase the investment made in them and others see no increase in what they were given. Having an 'at once' spirit is what will save your life and help you move forward because it makes you a doer not a dawdler. God is looking for people with an 'at once' spirit; he is looking for an 'at once' church and for 'at once' leaders.

If you have an 'at once' spirit it means that the talent you have is not going to remain in your hands longer than it should. You will use it, share it and give it away as soon as possible. I am a very excitable person which means that if I am excited about something, I want you to be excited too. I have to share everything with those close to me in my world. If it blesses me, why can't it bless them? On many occasions my husband has had to stop me calling my close friends in the middle of the night to tell them something I am excited about! He explains that they would rather share my enthusiasm in daylight rather than in the middle of their sleep. I just can't help it because I have discovered the joy of sharing. The day Hope Cherish was born was such a long awaited day and within hours of her arrival into the world we had shared our elation. She had been held and kissed by all my sisters within the first few moments of her life. The midwife commented that they don't usually have this many people in the delivery room, but I just couldn't help it, I had to share the joy.

I certainly don't want to save anything up or hold anything back. I want to give away all I can to help others. I have realized that an entrustment can only bring a return when it is invested in others. Since you have come to know God you have received much love, favour, wisdom, forgiveness and blessing. What have you done with it all? 'At once people' love to share their 'much' and don't keep it for themselves. These people have the ability to make things happen and produce a quick return.

What's in your cupboard?

I want to encourage you to examine your life. Stop saying, 'I've nothing to give' when you haven't even taken a proper look at what you've actually got. Your life is like a store cupboard and you were created with just the right size of cupboard, one which contains all the essential ingredients you need for your life. So it's time to open the doors, blow the dust off the tins that you haven't touched for years, empty each shelf and do a stock check of your life. You need to find out what's in your cupboard!

To help you believe just how much you have hidden away in there, here are some items that I have often found are sitting unused and forgotten in the cupboard of people's lives. There's the gift of friendship, which is always needed by someone; the gift of wisdom, which is often in short supply; and what about kindness and encouragement which everyone needs. Often we don't even consider these things as being gifts but there are people in your world right now whose lives could be transformed by you giving away that wisdom and kindness. It would be a life changing gift to them.

Thousands of cupboards overflowing with blessing are locked up; they are the equivalent of the talent buried in the ground, and I am on a mission to help open cupboards all over the world. Why? Because God will not let you get away with living a life with your doors tightly shut.

One mistake many people make is to think that their cupboard is poorly stocked in comparison to everyone else's, and by doing so devalue what God had given them.

Imagine that I gave you fifty pounds - I am sure you would be blessed by that! You may even go shopping to buy something you had been saving up for. Would you still feel the same way if I then gave the person next to you one hundred and fifty pounds? Most people would forget how grateful they were for the fifty pounds and immediately start thinking instead how unfair it was that they didn't get the one hundred and fifty.

Comparing will always rob you of your joy and make you devalue what God has entrusted to you. But we are not in a competition. The idea is that while you might have eggs, icing sugar and chocolate sprinkles, I have got flour and milk - and we need them all to get the cake made! Together we get the job done. We should not be comparing but complimenting each other. You need what I have got and I need what you have got. When God's people work together you see the full range of his gifts in action and you can get so much more done. So stop comparing yourself and use what you have been given.

SELL BY OR SELL OUT?

You need to have a sense of urgency about giving away what you have because some of what God has given you is perishable. It has a 'sell by' date on it and needs to be used within a certain amount of time. Just as food in your fridge can go off, the contents of your spiritual life cupboard can go stale if you leave them there for too long. If someone is going through a hard time, they need that word of encouragement from you today, not next week. The family who are struggling to make ends meet need that financial gift now, not later. That couple who are struggling in their marriage need your wisdom now, not when they are on the verge of separating! Check your life for odours. Usually they are a sign that something has been left in your cupboard for too long and is beginning to go off! It is a terrible waste of what God has given you if you leave it sitting there until it rots away.

When Steve and I were first married we regularly threw food away just because we hadn't got around to eating it (terrible I know!). We were out so much that we would end up grabbing a takeaway or eating at a friend's home. So some of the food we thought we would be in to eat, ended up in the bin. Having a baby has changed that because we are now in on an evening, we stay home more. Now the reverse is true, we have a constant stream of family and friends coming to our house because we can't go to theirs and they empty our fridge daily! So I am constantly having to replenish our food supplies and stock up more than ever before.

It's not about you

Now nothing is wasted in my food cupboard at home. In fact I have gone even further than that. In my food cupboard at home you will now find a stack of things I don't like and would never choose to eat. You will find rice pudding, marmalade, olives, teabags and Tabasco sauce. I don't like any of these things but they are not there for my benefit. The reason I have them in my cupboard is because I know that certain people in my world will one day drop by and want a cup of tea or a particular snack, so I keep things I know they enjoy. It should be the same with our spiritual cupboard; we keep things in stock just in case someone else needs them.

In my own life I have been through experiences that I haven't wanted to talk about. But I have come to realize that everything is in my cupboard for a reason and I can't pick and choose what I will let God use. There may be items in your cupboard that you don't like, there may be difficult circumstances you went through and don't want to be reminded of. You have moved on from that relationship that went wrong; you don't want to keep looking back at the time you backslid, and so on. But what you learned during those times are now valuable supplies you can use to help others.

BUILDING STOREHOUSES

The church is God's storehouse, it is where he has always chosen to place his 'much'. Although it has been filled to capacity with provisions that are desperately needed by the world, most of it has never been passed on. So no-one is asking much of the church anymore. When an unsaved person needs to ask for help they don't usually go to church to find it. But the church should be the first place they go to!

We need to commit to build churches that are not only storehouses for the family of God but that are also storehouses for our communities and the world.

I am glad to say that my home church is known across our city for being a place of 'much'. It has a reputation for having a fully stocked cupboard. People know that they can come to our storehouse and help themselves to wisdom, to acceptance, to forgiveness and a fresh start. They don't come just to empty the cupboards of the leaders, because they can find answers and provision from everyone they meet. From the young mum with three children, the smiling helper on the welcome team, through to the old lady in her nineties who is rich in wisdom. There are plenty of cupboards to choose from!

You will find that when people realise your church is a massive storehouse, and that its contents taste good, word will spread through your community. Then there will be an ever increasing level of demand coming in your direction.

So, we need to make sure that we are constantly well stocked. We need to live ready for the demand that will be made on God's entrustment to us.

Too many times I have seen and heard people express regret about things they wish they had said or done for someone who is no longer alive or in their sphere of influence. I have listened at memorial services where people pour out their expressions of love for the one they have lost. It would have been far better to say those kind words when they were still here but they missed their opportunity. I want to make sure that in my life I don't hold anything back. I want to let God prompt me to empty my cupboard at the right time and believe in the value of all he has placed in my life. So if you are reading this and you have been putting something off for a while, put this book down and go do it now.

God has high expectations of you because he knows the value of everything he has placed in your life. He will not settle for you living with a full cupboard and is sending people to your world to place a demand on you. Get ready because 'asking' is about to arrive in your world. It's time to empty your cupboard!

[1] Luke 12:48

[2] 2 Timothy 1:14

[3] Matthew 11:30

[4] Matthew 25:14-30

[5] Matthew 25:30

[6] Matthew 25:16

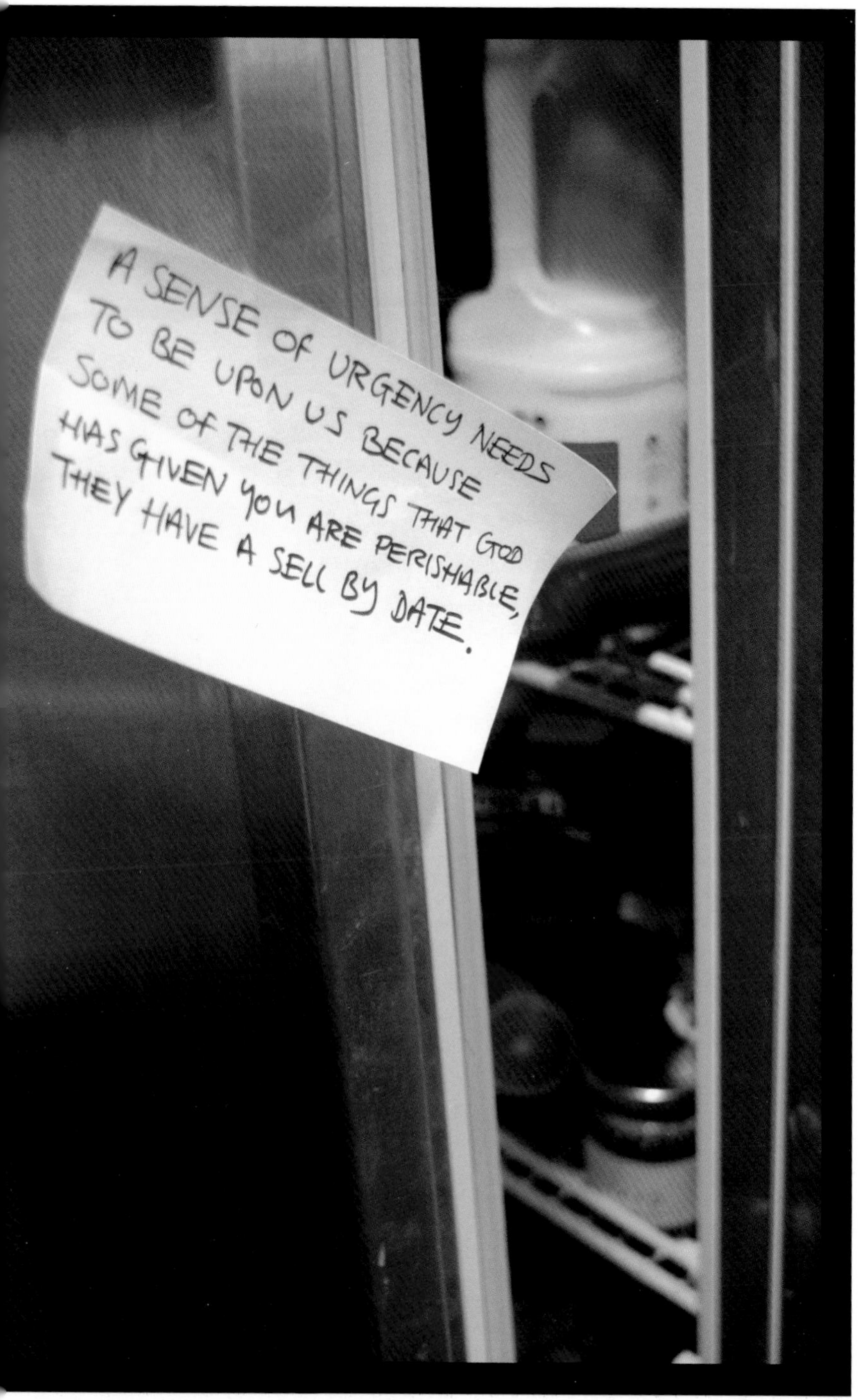
A SENSE OF URGENCY NEEDS
TO BE UPON US BECAUSE
SOME OF THE THINGS THAT GOD
HAS GIVEN YOU ARE PERISHABLE,
THEY HAVE A SELL BY DATE.

I HAVE FOUND ON MANY OCCASIONS
THAT THE ANSWER DOESN'T
NEED PULLING OUT OF HEAVEN,
BECAUSE IT IS ALREADY IN OUR MIDST.

CHAPTER 7

the culture of asking

Too many people are waiting for their big moment to use the 'much' that has been entrusted to them. They are waiting to be asked. Some are waiting for church leaders to recognize their giftedness and put them to work, longing for someone, anyone, to prophesy over them and confirm the call of God. But this is not the normal way God operates. The demand for what has been entrusted to you, more often than not, will not be accompanied by a big fanfare or a personal visitation from the angel Gabriel! It will more likely come as you go about your everyday life. In fact it is probably happening around you all the time but you just don't recognize it. The demand, which comes in the form of asking, comes from the people in your world; those you do life with, your family, your friends and your colleagues.

That is the way Jesus lived during his time on earth, even though he had so much wisdom, insight and power. Even though he could hold the attention of crowds for hours with his teaching ability, for Jesus this was secondary to his love for helping people. He was not obsessed with what he wanted to say but placed a high priority on what people needed to hear by answering their questions. He had a ministry that was highly interruptible. He spoke people's language and was happy to tackle the questions that religion had failed to answer. He would even answer the most obvious of questions that the disciples asked him. I am sure sometimes he felt there were greater things he could be doing and saying, deeper truth he could be expounding but for him the importance was giving an answer to every heart felt question.

Jesus came to earth to provide answers for the world. He gave acceptance and forgiveness to the woman at the well not a lecture, he gave healing to those who were sick not a sermon, he gave sight to the blind and food to the hungry. It was a simple exchange, what they asked for he supplied. Dealing with Jesus was not complicated. He explained it this way: '*Which of you fathers if your son asks for a fish, will give him a snake instead? Or if he asks for an egg, will give him a scorpion? If you then, though you are evil, know how to give good gifts to your children, how much more will your Father in heaven give the Holy Spirit to those who ask him?*' [1]

With Jesus, what you asked for was what you got. How refreshing! So often in church life we don't ask for what we really want and more often than not we don't respond with the answer someone needs. That is something we must address.

Not only vertical

Asking is not only supposed to be vertical - something exclusively between us and God - it is also meant to be horizontal, between us and those we do life with. This is the dimension I think we have lost in the church today.

Some people spend months praying for God to help them when the answer is sitting three rows behind them in church each week! It is in the form of a couple who have a cupboard full of wisdom. Yet we don't ask them for help and so in turn they never give away what they have, thinking it is not needed.

The book of Acts provides a glimpse into the DNA of the first church. The first ever group of believing Believers were an 'asking church'. This incredible church was increasing in number daily and this was in no small part due to the fact that they had developed a culture of asking. Yet I have never read a church growth manual that has talked about 'asking' as a key to growing a church - but it so evidently was. I believe that an asking church is an irresistible church.

We need to cultivate that same culture in our churches today and recapture that same essence of giving that was evident among those early believers. It is a culture that encourages you to ask for help without fear or embarrassment, a culture that encourages everyone to help meet each other's needs, and a culture where everyone is honest about where they are at. That culture was prevalent in the early church because they liberated people to ask.

We read, '*All the believers were together and had everything in common. Selling their possessions and goods they gave to anyone as he had need.*' [2] The early church weren't expecting God to miraculously drop all the answers they needed from heaven, because they had discovered that many of their daily needs could be met by sharing what they already had. In the same way, we also need to start opening our eyes to see what God has placed in the lives of those around us; often they already have what we need. You need to know that God is not going to send you milk supernaturally when you are short of it when your friend owns a cow! He has already provided you with an answer. You need to go and ask for it!

I am convinced that many churches have got far too complicated when it comes to meeting the needs of those in their congregation and the community beyond. There are far fewer things we have to pull out of heaven with our prayers than we think because, more often than not, the answer is already in our midst. After all, Peter tells us that '*His divine power has given us everything we need for life and godliness.*' [3] If we really believe this, then we need to spend less time looking up and more time looking around.

Recently we had a large donation made towards a building

project we are involved in as a church. This generous gift moved me deeply, not because of the amount but because of the circumstances surrounding the person who had given it. It came from an ex-convict and drug dealer who is now in our church. This young guy who is now saved and successful in business, had an answer to our need. Yet I asked myself that day, how many people would have loved, accepted and been prepared to meet his asking if he'd first joined their church? He came to us with a lot of questions, he needed a lot of help, love and forgiveness. But the culture of our House gave him the freedom to ask. He asked our House for help and we gave it. Now several years later he is giving in response to our asking. How awesome is that! Sadly, many want the miracle money but don't want to spend time answering the demanding questions that preceded it.

The problem is that many of us are either too embarrassed, scared or intimidated to ask for help. I remember hating French lessons when I was at school. It wasn't because I didn't want to learn a different language, or that I couldn't speak some French. I hated my French lessons because of the culture the teacher had created in the classroom. She created the impression that if we asked a question, it meant we were stupid. She told us it was a sign that we were not listening and therefore we were wasting her time. Throughout the entire lesson she refused to speak English and we were only allowed to speak in French. If you dared to ask a question in English she made you stand in the corner of the classroom inside the dustbin and would say, 'that is where rubbish belongs!' After my third lesson standing in the garbage bin, I remember telling my parents why I really didn't enjoy French. No sooner had I recounted my experience and my dad was on his way to the school to ask a few questions of his own. Needless to say, I was never put in the bin again! Many people, though they may not have had the same classroom experience I endured, have been made to feel the same way if they have a question.

There is a culture in society that can be very intimidating, a culture which implies that asking a question is a sign of weakness and speaking up about your need for help is an embarrassment. Unfortunately, this culture has entered the House of God and it has no place there. Sadly many people in church life feel too intimidated to ask questions. From the newest convert who dare not ask where Habakkuk is for fear of looking like they don't read their Bible, to the teenager who dare not ask about the pressure he is under to compromise his values morally for fear of being marked a disgraceful sinner, to the couple in leadership whose marriage is in desperate need of help, but they are too intimidated to ask for fear of looking like failures. I could go on but you get the point. Where is the culture of the Acts church where, if you had a need, you simply asked for help?

If asking is going to be part of the fabric and DNA of our churches, it must begin in the heart of the leaders. Recently, I was with our Leadership Academy students running a question and answer session as we often do. One of the students raised her hand and said, 'I want you to know that many of us can't think of anything to ask right now. You have already answered most of our questions by being so open and honest; just being here answers our questions.' She was saying that the culture of the church had already answered her questions, it was open, transparent and an environment where answers were easy to find.

Leaders have the key role in shaping the culture of their church. They determine the atmosphere and set the thermostat for that 'greenhouse'. So, for leaders to create this culture they must empower people to ask one another for help. It means empowering them to ask each other for help instead of always having to go to the pastor, their home group leader or youth worker for advice. Controlling leaders often struggle with this, they like people to come to them, they want to know exactly what is going on in every area of church life and they like to have all the answers to give. It is potentially very intimidating to have to queue to see the pastor to find out if it is OK to take the job, date the girl or move house – but it happens. I know of a church where the leaders regularly pray over a couple's photographs and have to feel a peace from the Lord before they are even allowed to go on a date!

If asking is going to be part of the fabric of a church, its leaders must take responsibility for liberating the people. This means that as leaders they must be open, honest and willing to relinquish control. It means ceasing to believe that they are the only ones with all the answers simply because they are the leaders.

There is a danger to be noted here. Sometimes leaders have made people's asking of them an indication of just how necessary they are. This asking feeds in them a sense of importance and affirms their leadership position. This is dangerous and leads to unhealthy dependencies. However, releasing people to ask others rather than you will remove these dangers. It means however, that people may at times make mistakes, they may give bad advice and they may not answer as perfectly as you would. But the benefits far outweigh the risks.

The problem for a lot of leaders is that their small thinking and their small church size has made them operate as a 'one man band'. Everybody asks the pastor because everybody can. But we must build our churches with the future in mind. Ask yourself, if thousands were added, where would they get answers? Just think about what was happening to the early church. It was growing at a rapid rate, people were being added daily, so there was simply no way all those people could be helped unless they looked after each other. If your church experienced this type of exponential growth I think you would quickly start looking around for people who could help. Well, why wait for a problem before you empower people? Dare to believe in the capability of those around you now and liberate them to be part of the answer.

BE REAL

We have noted that intimidation locks up churches and stops people asking questions. Linked to this is another huge contributing factor, pride. People simply don't ask because they are too proud and therefore embarrassed. They are lost, yet refuse to ask directions from others who they know are further along on the same road. They have simply forgotten how to be real. How sad that they are too embarrassed to ask for help and would rather drive for hours in the wrong direction than risk the humiliation of people knowing just how lost they actually are.

What is it about men and asking for directions in particular? What joy do they find in remaining lost? We ladies are generally much more likely to pull over and ask for help if we are lost – but the guys? Never! Enough said on that one but I'm sure you get my point! Pride can be a huge hindrance to asking. Yet the truth is we all need to turn this around and instead of seeing asking as a sign of weakness, we should celebrate it as a sign of security and strength. A healthy church is an honest church. It's a church where people are real!

Our church staff offices overlook the car park and on numerous occasions I've watched as couples get out of their cars while in mid-flow of a very animated argument. They are trying their best to control their unruly children. Then suddenly the scene changes as others walk past and engage their attention. Now the arguing couple are smiling at each other whilst patting the children on the head, albeit very firmly! They disguise their dysfunction and put on a great Christian performance. But church is supposed to be your home. It should be the place where you are the real you, warts and all.

For instance, in my home I never wear shoes because I much prefer to go barefoot. I drink out of cartons from the fridge, because I can't be bothered to wash up the glass. Home is where I put my feet on the furniture and paint my toe-nails over the cream carpet - when my husband is not looking! I am just Charlotte, I am myself because it's my home and it is where I am most comfortable.

So why do people feel such a pressure to be something they are not when they come home to God's House? If it is your home you need to be the real you and let others help you deal with whatever is going on in your world. We need to have churches where we can be real with one another, places where we can ask for what we really need without fear of being judged, ridiculed or gossiped about.

When we create a culture of asking in the church it encourages people to be real. Church then becomes a safe place where they can be honest about their lives because they aren't expected to be perfect. We also start to look at others differently and no longer base our belief in them on what we see, but on Christ's belief in them. He always sees beyond our current weaknesses and struggles because he knows our future and sees the person we will become.

A while ago I sat talking to one of the women in our church. She was someone I had been taking time to invest and believe in because I saw so much potential in her world. That day she had asked if she could come and share her testimony with me, there were some things she had been hiding away in her cupboard. As we talked, she shared how she and her husband had been through some really difficult times. There had been adultery in the marriage and she had ended up suicidal and completely at the end of herself as she tried to deal with this crisis while caring for her young children. Since that time God had restored their relationship but people in the church had no idea about the struggles they had been through. She knew this experience was in her cupboard and the culture in the church, of believing in each other and being real, had stirred her heart to be open about it.

This amazing couple are now helping others by the power of their testimony. I have often wondered how many people would not have benefited from their experience if they hadn't felt able to share it. I thank them and the many people around the world like them who are willing to give their life away no matter how difficult it is for them personally. They are believing Believers who share their stories because they believe enough in God's forgiveness, and in their entrustment, to use what they have been through to bless others.

BE SPECIFIC

Developing a culture of asking means that we start to place a demand on the lives of those around us. We actively start looking to see what is in each other's cupboards and ask for it. We will start to believe in each other's potential to help, we will honour each other's wisdom and by doing so, cause people to give from what they have been entrusted with. Their giving will then produce growth, both in the life of the asker and in the one who is answering.

Too many people fail to understand that every demand placed on them will grow them, no matter where the asking comes from. So when it arrives in the form of a familiar face they ignore it because it doesn't quite look how they had imagined. It seems far too ordinary and unspiritual. Instead they sit back waiting for their dream opportunity or for their pastor or leaders to ask them to do something that will raise their profile.

I know that every significant growth opportunity in my life has come from a friend, someone close to me who has seen in me some potential ability or gift and asked me to use it. The first time I ever served in church I did not hear a voice from heaven saying 'This is your moment Charlotte, this is what you are called to do.' It was far more ordinary than that. Someone just came to me and said they needed help in Kid's Church and thought I would be great as I loved kids. There were no flashing lights to confirm this was a God idea, no angels, no goose-bumps, just a simple request for me to give something away. It was the same the first time I spoke in house group, it was the same the first time I led worship and it has been the same ever since.

When I was younger I remember asking my dad for some money to go to the cinema. I asked for five pounds thinking it was an acceptable amount for what I needed and felt pleased with myself when I got what I asked for. But when my younger sister Beth produced a twenty pound note that Dad had just given her, I was angry. I complained that I had only been given five pounds and her reply was, 'It's not my fault, you should have asked for more!' And she was right. Many Christians live life like this, they are not specific about what they want so they always receive less than what they actually needed.

Many people reduce their asking to a ministry of hints because they refuse to be real. They only hint at what they need and this is hard work for everyone involved. Their friends and those they do life with end up getting caught in a time consuming guessing game. Be warned, none of us are mind readers, we don't instantly know that, 'It's been a tough week but I'll just keep soldiering on,' actually means 'I really need some advice about my kids, they are driving me crazy and I am at breaking point.' We don't know that, 'My husband is really busy at work right now,' actually means, 'My husband is never home and we are rapidly drifting apart.'

If someone tells me that he has had a bit of a row with his wife then my advice might be to apologise and give her some flowers. But if the truth is that this couple haven't spoken for three months and are sleeping in separate bedrooms then a bunch of flowers isn't going to help! The situation is way past making romantic gestures, they need more help than that. But I can only release the wisdom they need into their world if they ask for what they really need!

Please don't inflict your hinting on those around you because there is nothing more frustrating than trying to guess what someone wants. If you need a twenty pound answer don't ask for five pounds worth of wisdom. It creates a problem not just for you but also for the people who are trying to respond.

So, we need the church today to model what we have observed in the early church of the book of Acts. The power of belief that people had in each other was a great empowerment and the constant demand they placed on each other motivated them to keep opening their cupboards to meet many of the needs that were around them. These believing Believers were not content to sit around and wait for answers from heaven because they understood what they had already been entrusted with by God. They could help to eradicate need by responding to each other's asking. We also need a House where, because everyone freely asks, we eradicate need.

[1] Luke 11:11-13

[2] Acts 2:45

[3] 2 Peter 1:3

A HEALTHY CHURCH IS AN
HONEST CHURCH – IT'S A
CHURCH WHERE PEOPLE ARE REAL
Dr Gillian McKeith
Dr Ali's Weight Loss
SOUTH BEACH DIET Cookbook

YOU NEED FRIENDS WHO ARE HAPPY TO INCONVENIENCE YOU, THEY WILL SEE PAST YOUR RELUCTANCE AND DEMAND THAT YOU RESPOND.

CHAPTER 8

lend me your loaf

Before we embark on liberating a culture of asking in our lives and churches, and empower all those in our world to ask for what they need, we must be aware that asking is only part of the equation. It has a travelling companion that must accompany it. The culture of asking will only work if it finds a heart that is willing to respond. Therefore, just as much work, if not more, needs to go into creating an environment where people are prepared to respond willingly. Where these two companions are not found together, you will have people who are great at asking but are very weak at extending answers to anyone else. It is one way traffic; their life becomes a cul-de-sac of wisdom, a dead-end alley. Our challenge therefore, is to make sure that we ask and we answer with the same amount of enthusiasm.

One of the major hindrances to a responsive life is the handbrake of reluctance. Just as you think about responding, your reluctance to get up and provide the answer needed overwhelms you. The truth is your thought doesn't count. Thinking about answering is no replacement for actually responding. There are lots of people who want to help but wanting to help and actually helping are two different matters entirely. Many churches have become docile and slow because they have allowed the sleeping pill of reluctance to enter the life of their church. Unnoticed and unchallenged, it has been allowed to create a huge chasm of delay between those asking and the response they need.

The reason many are slow to respond, is that they are not in control of the timing or the level of demand that the one asking places upon them. Too many churches have become so preoccupied with their own programmes and meetings that they simply haven't the time to stop and answer other people's requests for help. They are too busy with their own initiatives to take notice of the needs of those around them. If we want people to come to our churches, if we want growth, then we need to lose our reluctance and embrace the demand that asking will bring. We must cultivate a responsive heart.

Jesus once told a parable about the tension between an asker and a responder. In this story the person responding was less than enthusiastic, they were reluctant and they were unwilling to help their friend:

'Then he said to them, "Suppose one of you has a friend, and he goes to him at midnight and says, 'Friend, lend me three loaves of bread, because a friend of mine on a journey has come to me, and I have nothing to set before him.' "Then the one inside answers, 'Don't bother me. The door is already locked, and my children are with me in bed. I can't get up and give you anything.' "I tell you, though he will not get up and give him the bread because he is his friend, yet because of the man's boldness he will get up and give him as much as he needs."' [1]

This man was his friend's only hope in the middle of the night. There was no 24-hour supermarket option, he had to rely on those in his world to help! Yet his friend's response must have made this man feel even more embarrassed and troubled than he already was.

The friend in this story was a reluctant responder. He was reluctant to wake up, he was reluctant to get out of bed and he was reluctant to hand over anything from his cupboard that night. At first all he was willing to hand over was a list of pitiful excuses to explain why he couldn't help. He said, *'Don't bother me. The door is already locked, and my children are with me in bed. I can't get up and give you anything.'*

INCONVENIENCE

You need to face the fact that asking is never convenient. You can be sure that it will not come when you have a night off, it will not come during a spare half hour and it will not come when you have nothing better to do. It is more likely that you will be busy with a long list of other priorities when it lands. I am sure that when the man in this story heard the knock at the door, he thought, why me? Why now at midnight? Why three loaves? Why couldn't this wait until the morning?

Yet the reality is that you can't control what people want or what people need. You can't tell them, 'three o'clock next Wednesday is clear in my diary so can you hold your need until then?' If someone is banging on your door at midnight, causing such a disturbance that they have woken you and the entire neighbourhood, then there will be a good reason for it! We need to deliver one another from having to cause a scene; it doesn't need to go that far. You can respond at the first knock or you can make somebody wear themselves out from banging when they really need your help. The choice lies in the heart of the responder. So, if you want to respond to the demands placed on your life you need to know that it will be inconvenient. You have no control over what you will be asked, you cannot choose when you will be asked and you have no say in how often people will ask.

Jesus was someone who understood this. I don't think you

or I will ever have the same level of demand placed on us as he had. Wherever he went people were asking from his life. I am sure it was often inconvenient but he always had a response and an answer. He said, 'Give to the one who asks you, and do not turn away from the one who wants to borrow from you.'² That was the way he lived his life, always willing to respond to people who wanted to place a demand on his life.

Have you ever wondered why Jesus' first miracle was turning water into wine? Well I have! Out of all the amazing miracles he could have begun his ministry with, why this one? I would have thought that as the Son of God he would have gone for something far more spectacular with a much bigger 'wow' factor and in front of more people than a few wedding guests. I believe the answer lies in his willingness to be a responder, he simply could not resist answering the questions from those around when he knew he had the answer inside him.

The scripture says that 'On the third day a wedding took place at Cana in Galilee. Jesus' mother was there, and Jesus and his disciples had also been invited to the wedding. When the wine was gone, Jesus' mother said to him, "They have no more wine." "Dear woman, why do you involve me?" Jesus replied. "My time has not yet come." His mother said to the servants, "Do whatever he tells you."' ³

Reading this makes me think that Jesus did not go to the wedding intending to perform his first miracle. He was just there as a guest, hanging out with the other disciples but then he had a 'mum moment'. His mother, who knew him and what he was capable of, came and asked for something from him. And she wasn't willing to take no for an answer!

She could have just ignored the problem, she could have deflected the request for help, or she could have pointed them in the direction of the nearest vineyard because she didn't want the inconvenience. But she was not reluctant or slow to respond. She went straight to Jesus because she knew he could help. I imagine she went to him and said 'I know this isn't quite what you had planned, and it is a bit ahead of schedule. I know this is probably not the way you wanted to launch your ministry – but these people are friends of mine and it is embarrassing for them to have run out of wine. We don't want the bride to be in tears on her wedding day do we?'

I can imagine him saying, 'But Mother, it's not the right time for me yet. Making alcohol is not the best way of unveiling my miracle working power. It's a bit controversial don't you think?'

I don't think that Mary sat pondering all the options that day. She didn't need to because she knew Jesus had the answer and he wouldn't withhold what he knew he had. Their sense of urgency to get an answer far outweighed the inconvenience of the situation.

DISTURBING FRIENDSHIPS

You need friends in your world like Mary, friends who will inconvenience you, friends who won't leave you alone or be put off by your unenthusiastic response.

You need friends like the man in the parable who press past inconvenience and stay on the doorstep knocking. You need friends who will not accept your reluctance or be easily put off. They will provoke you to keep on giving. If you are a leader then you need to disturb the people in your church, you need to keep on challenging them to keep growing and giving, to keep going beyond where they have been before. You need to eradicate reluctance from your world.

Many people don't want to be bothered by the requests of others, so instead of developing 'disturbing friendships' they develop something far less demanding. They form relationships that are purely social and not very beneficial to their world. The friendships they build are shallow and have no depth to them. Their hearts are not joined together and their destinies are not linked. They may be having fun socialising but no one is growing, no one is changing, and no one is being challenged.

I have made sure that I have some very disturbing friends. It might seem like a really strange thing to say, but it's the truth. My friends will just not leave me alone; they are always asking for something out of my cupboard, wanting to borrow my loaf. They come round to my house at those midnight moments and place a demand on me. This might sound like hard work to you, but it is what we have purposely built into our friendship. If you want to get out of you what is inside, you need disturbing friends in your world. People who will say to you, 'I know you have what I need in your cupboard, please give it to me!' This type of friend will not let you get away with a stinking attitude, they will not let you settle for doing less than they know you are capable of. Your pitiful excuses of why you can't help them just won't work and they give you no option but to start emptying your cupboard!

A great story about the difference disturbing friends can make to your world is found in Mark where we read:

'A few days later, when Jesus again entered Capernaum, the people heard that he had come home. So many gathered that there was no room left, not even outside the door, and he preached the word to them. Some men came, bringing to him a paralytic, carried by four of them. Since they could not get him to Jesus because of the crowd, they made an opening in the roof above Jesus and, after digging through it, lowered the mat the paralyzed man was lying on. When Jesus saw their faith, he said to the paralytic, "Son, your sins are forgiven."' [4]

I can imagine that many people went to that house needing a touch from Jesus. I am sure that this man was not the only paralytic who wanted to walk again, but that day he got his heart's desire. The only reason for it was the disturbing friends he had in his world. I am sure that when they turned up at his house that morning saying, 'come on, we are taking you to Jesus', he thought up a whole host of reasons why it couldn't be done! He probably argued with them saying, 'I can't get there, I'll never get through the crowd, it's not going to work!'

His friends had other ideas and wherever there was a potential problem they found a solution. Without them he had no way of leaving his house because he couldn't walk, so they gave him the option of being carried. Once he got there he could not get near to Jesus because of the crowds of people, so they gave him the option of being lowered down through the roof by making a hole in it! They went past every excuse and pushed past every barrier and simply would not take no for an answer. Their belief created new options for his life and opened up new possibilities.

Disturbing friends believe in you and it is the power of their belief that can add momentum to your life and help keep you going. They just won't let you quit, they won't let you settle for a second rate life when God has called you to so much more. The way they provoke you to do more isn't always comfortable. I am sure the paralytic did not feel at ease being lowered through a hole in someone's roof to queue jump the thousands of people hoping to meet Jesus that day! His believing friends did it because they refused to give up on him, they wanted him to be healed. Their persistence and willingness to disturb Jesus made his miracle healing possible.

PERSISTENCE

The friends of the paralytic had a certain quality in their lives that took them past the ordinary and made them do things that were not usual or expected. Their persistence was what caused them to go beyond the expected and start digging a hole in the roof of that house. They were believing Believers and if you have a deep belief in your world it makes you persistent as a person. When belief takes root in your heart it will not move, it will not be shaken and it will not fade. It brings with it an immovable determination so that even when people around you give up, you just keep on going. Your belief in God's Word makes you keep on putting one foot after another to continue on your journey. It says in James that, *the testing of your faith develops perseverance*, [5] and when your believing has been tested it becomes a far more potent force in your life because you know its worth, you know it is real. It gives you the faith to persist!

Jesus said, *Ask and it will be given to you; seek and you will find; knock and the door will be opened to you.* [6] Some people don't have this type of determination in their lives. They are easy to refuse, they don't argue with you and they don't hassle you, they just take 'no' for an answer. But others are different in their approach. If they know you have got something they need they will ask you, harangue you, and bother you about it until they persuade you to hand it over. They keep asking, they keep seeking and they keep on knocking until they get a result. This is the mark of a persistent person and persistency manages to draw things out of people's lives that they would not otherwise have given up.

Jesus once told a story about a widow who had mastered the art of persistence. This extraordinary lady had a question and was not afraid to ask and to keep on asking until she got her answer! '*In a certain town there was a judge who neither feared God nor cared about men. And there was a widow in that town who kept coming to him with the plea, "Grant me justice against my adversary." For some time he refused. But finally he said to himself, "Even though I don't fear God or care about men, yet because this widow keeps bothering me, I will see that she gets justice, so that she won't eventually wear me out with her coming!"*' [7]

This widow took on the judge, a man people feared and someone who didn't believe in her God. What chance would she have of persuading him to help her? But she had a secret weapon that was able to disarm his reluctance, she had persistency! I can just imagine him looking over his shoulder every time he left his house to check she wasn't following him again, he just couldn't escape her and in the end he couldn't ignore her pleas any longer. When the judge gave her the answer she wanted, it wasn't because he was concerned for her, neither was it because he wanted to see justice done, the only reason he got involved was because she had become an irritation to his life. In the same way, sometimes the things you need in your world will only come through your preparedness to be regarded as an irritation to the people who you know have an answer. Persistence is always purposeful, it has a reason, but nagging is just moaning. And being persistent is the only way you will get some of the answers you desperately need.

THE BORROWERS

After reading this chapter it may seem like you are going to have an endless stream of people wanting a whole list of things from your life. It can sound like a whole lot of hard work. So, you need to get God's perspective on this. When we help someone by passing on what they need in their world, we are handing them a valuable gift that they can then pass on to others in the future. You are starting a ripple effect as they pass your wisdom to the next person and on it travels. You just don't know where it will end up!

My daughter Hope went through a stage where everything was a question. She repeatedly asked 'Why? Why?' And 'What's that?' It drove me to distraction after a while. All our car journeys became a game of question and answer. Every minute began to feel like an hour of interrogation. No sooner did I explain to her what a tree was and what grass was and she asked the same question again and again. Then one day we were driving in the car and she pointed out of the window and said, 'Mummy, that's a tree'. She had been borrowing that word from me for a while but then one day she got it, the penny dropped, she had learned something new and now that knowledge had become her own. That is how it works in all our lives.

Asking is necessary to growth and if we don't have a willingness to respond then we rob people of the opportunity to learn and move on. The immature question that you are avoiding answering will only create a bigger problem because you are preventing that person from growing. The more questions we are willing to answer, the more knowledge we pass on and the more growth we facilitate in the people we empower. We will all go through seasons where we have to ask. I thank God for every person in my world who moved past reluctance and gave me an answer – that is how healthy a church grows.

Doesn't it feel great when you can answer someone's question? It was like that for me with Hope because I already knew what trees and grass were! But I dread the day she comes home with algebra homework because the right answers are not in my cupboard! So I'm enjoying this stage while I can. In the same way we need to enjoy the fact that we know some stuff and be willing to put our hands up and say, 'Let me lend you my loaf!'

So, don't keep asking God for an opportunity when one is already knocking on your door at midnight for a loaf. Many people reason their destiny away like this; they just don't recognize that the person making a demand on them was sent by God. It all starts with getting out of bed, unlocking the door and helping your friend.

[1] Luke 11:5-8

[2] Matthew 5:42

[3] John 2:1-5

[4] Mark 2:1-5

[5] James 1:3

[6] Luke 11:9

[7] Luke 18:2-5

There simply isn't any time to be wasted and that is why God is looking for believing believers.

CHAPTER 9

your time is up

I n this book I have talked a lot about belief. I have tried to take you on a journey to find out what you truly believe and to identify the evidence of it being outworked in your life.

My prayer is that every Believer reading this book becomes a believing Believer; someone who doesn't just believe things about God but truly believes in God and what he says, because that is the only way to find a life that gives true fulfillment. It is the only way to bring closeness and intimacy into your walk with him. God gets involved in the lives of believing Believers in a special way. There is something about your 'first following' and your 'doing' that he is highly attracted to. Being a believing Believer will open up your horizons and allow you to see a lot more opportunities which the blinkers of doubt and unbelief have screened out of your sight until now. Being a believing Believer delivers you from living under the intimidation of people who may place their opinion and expectations on you. They may wrongly try to load things into your life. But believing in God's entrustment and recognising what he has put in the cupboard of your life liberates you to get busy making the most of what you have.

Once the truth of God's Word begins to take root in your heart and comes alive in you, it will change the way you see the world. It is so important we put this living, breathing, belief to work because there is so much to do, and no one person or no one church can do it all. We need the contents of everybody's cupboard if we are going to impact this generation and leave a legacy for those following behind. There are so many people to be reached, so many broken lives to be restored, so many churches that need to be built in a way that will attract the world by their vibrant expression of God's life. There simply isn't any time to be wasted and that is why God is looking for believing Believers.

WHERE ARE THE FIGS?

Before I finish, I want to challenge you with this story. Jesus told a parable about a fig tree that was barren. The tree had nothing to show for the time it had spent in the soil it was planted in. Jesus' attitude towards this fruitless fig tree could be seen as severe, but after all you have just read, I hope you will understand more about where the urgency in the Father's heart comes from:

'A man had a fig tree, planted in his vineyard, and he went to look for fruit on it, but did not find any. So he said to the man who took care of the vineyard, "For three years now I've been coming to look for fruit on this fig tree and haven't found any. Cut it down! Why should it use up the soil?"
"Sir," the man replied, "leave it alone for one more year, and I'll dig around it and fertilize it. If it bears fruit next year, fine! If not, then cut it down."' [1]

What God has given you is on loan, it came with expectations. He therefore, has every right to come looking for figs if he created you to produce them. Just like the owner in this parable, God is coming to your life. It is not a case of he might come, or maybe if he can fit you in, he will come. He is definitely coming to your life and to mine to ask, 'where are the figs?' Therefore we need to get ready to give our answer because God will not be satisfied with excuses.

The question the master asked of the fig tree wasn't unfair because he wasn't asking for anything beyond the tree's ability. God isn't being unreasonable, he places a demand on your life for the things he knows you are capable of producing. The owner in the parable didn't say, 'Fig tree, where are the oranges? I demand oranges from your life.' He asked for figs. So, if God is asking where your figs are it is because he knows they are in your cupboard. He is not teasing you, he isn't testing you with a question you have no possible way of answering. God will never ask for things he knows you don't have. He has a complete inventory of the stock in your cupboard, and he knows what is in there better than you. Maybe it is something that has been in your cupboard so long that you had forgotten about it, but now God is calling time on that testimony, on that wisdom and on that contribution.

Some people have stopped producing fruit because they have lost sight of the need for what they are carrying. They have become planted in a successful orchard and have lulled themselves into thinking that because everyone else around them has branches full of ripe fruit, there is no need for them to produce anything. They think that everyone else's 'much' will compensate for their lack.

Often when people join our church they can feel like this because of its size. I have seen them take a back seat for a while, thinking no-one will miss their time, serving or involvement. And the truth is that in a large church it can be true because people tend to come and go from the fringes of church life. But if that is your excuse for not producing anything, you are misunderstanding the whole point. Your fruit, your talent does not belong to me, I am not going to come and hold you accountable for it, but God is!

In this parable the fig tree was given grace for three years. It was allowed to enjoy the same soil as everyone else. It was loved, watered, pruned and fed all the right nutrients. It was exposed to all the same conditions as the other trees but eventually there came a time when that tree had to give back. The farmer came and warned the fig tree about the growing frustration of the vineyard owner. He let the fig tree know that its days were numbered if it didn't start producing. Its roots would be pulled up and its place in the soil given to another. It had one more chance; one more year to produce fruit or the axe would fall.

FRUIT-BEARING IS A PROCESS

After reading this you may be looking at your life and asking, 'Where are the figs?' You may be worried that there is simply not enough to show for your believing. The vineyard owner in this parable gave the fig tree time to produce fruit. He didn't say I'm coming back tomorrow, you must produce figs by eleven o'clock or I'm chopping you down. Growing fruit is not an overnight phenomena, it is a process and God is gracious enough to give you the time you need. It may be that after reading this book you have found areas of unbelief in your life and you have identified areas that you need to change. Unbelief will always stunt your growth, it will stop you producing quality fruit in your life. You need to dig up every root of it from your life and start to take charge of the conditions you are growing in. Make sure you are planted in great soil and regularly water yourself with God's Word. If you commit to this you will see fruit, because believing God will always bring a harvest.

As I have written this book I have felt a bit like that farmer. I have felt a growing sense of urgency and an emphasis in my spirit to say to some of you, 'you've got one more chance'. The master is coming and he is expecting to see figs.

Maybe this book will do for you what the farmer tried to do

for the fig tree; maybe this is digging around the soil of your life and unearthing some treasure that you had forgotten were under the top few inches of soil. If it is you I am talking to, then don't let another year slip by. Maybe God is going to give you a few more years but equally he may be giving you a few more days to get out what is in you before he gives the opportunity, favour and blessing that you have been sitting on to someone else.

I have been amazed how some people can be planted in God's House and flourish while others seem to take root but their life produces nothing. Yet the soil is the same! So the problem must be inside their lives. If you are not producing figs then you are violating your mandate and God is on your case. Whether you are battling with unbelief, struggling with doubts, held back by reluctance or just too embarrassed to ask for help, I have tried to give you ways to move your life forward in this book. So now you are left with a choice, to either give in and settle for life as an unbelieving Believer, or believe that your life has got something unique that the world desperately needs and only you have the power to give away.

I believe in you, all of heaven believes in you, many of the people you do life with believe in you. The question is, do you believe in you?

 Luke 13:6-9

I believe in you,
all of heaven believes in you,
many of the people you do life with believe in you,
but do you believe in you?

IN CLOSING…

I hope this book has provoked you to believe what God says about you, that it has challenged you to believe in yourself and to invest that power of belief in others.

If we truly are 'believing Believers', it will be expressed; we will be doing things that demonstrate our faith in action!

The following pages are about three amazing ministries that exist to pass on the gift of belief to others. They practically express to hurting people just how much God and other people value and believe in them. These ministries are changing lives around the world.

If you have something in the cupboard of your life that you want to give to support their work, please contact them using the details provided.

MERCY

'Mercy is an awesome ministry I believe in. I have known Nancy Alcorn, the founder of Mercy Ministries for a number of years and it has been an honour to have been involved in the birth of the first Mercy home in the UK.

Mercy loves to take some of societies' most broken women. It believes in their potential and creates a safe environment where God can lovingly restore them to live the lives he purposed for them. I encourage you to join with me in supporting this valuable work.'

Charlotte Scanlon-Gambill

Mercy Ministries provides residential support for women struggling with depression, drug and alcohol abuse, eating disorders, victims of physical or sexual abuse and unplanned pregnancy. Care is given free of charge and includes practical training in areas such as budgeting, nutrition and fitness as well as specific Christian counselling for each girl's needs. Together, we see these beautiful young women emerge confident and full of hope for the future.

Mercy Ministries operates homes in America, Asia Pacific and the UK.

Mercy Ministries UK, www.mercyministries.co,uk
Leeds House, 4 James Street, Bradford, West Yorkshire, Tel: 01274 745427

Mercy Ministries Asia Pacific www.mercyministries.com/au
PO Box 1537 Castle Hill, NSW 1765, Australia. Tel: 1800 011 537

Mercy Ministries of America www.mercyministries.com
PO Box 111060, Nashville, TN 37222-1060, USA Tel: (615) 831 6987

Compassion is a Christian child development agency providing individuals the opportunity to respond to the needs of the poor in a personal, practical and thoroughly Christian way.

They take children living in extreme poverty and with the support of individual sponsors, provide them with all they need to develop physically, socially, emotionally and spiritually. Whilst children are the greatest victims of poverty, they also hold the greatest potential to break the cycle of deprivation for future generations.

Compassion is Christ centred, child focused and church based in all it does. Through partnership with local churches, Compassion empowers Christians to reach out to children in desperate need with the love of God. Sponsors play a vital role not only in supporting a child financially, but also through letters of encouragement and prayers.

Compassion sponsored children often grow up to become change-makers in their communities. As pastors, teachers, doctors, nurses and engineers they powerfully impact the community in which they grew up.

Sponsoring a child with Compassion costs just £18 a month, which is barely 60p a day, but the significance of this will be immense. When you transform a child in Jesus' name you begin to change the world.

To start the life changing experience of sponsorship please visit www.compassionuk.org, e-mail info@compassionuk.org or call 01932 836495

The theme of the 2004 Cherish Conference for women was 'I Believe in You', and it was there that God placed in my heart the idea to launch the Cherish Foundation as a practical expression of the message we were preaching. It is a way of saying to women everywhere, 'God believes in you, and we believe in you!'

The Foundation exists to bless and honour women nominated by churches from across the Body of Christ. These are women who have overcome particular adversity in their lives, thinking more of others than themselves and often at great personal sacrifice.

God really loves these women! And it is now our joy as a Foundation to be the practical expression of his belief by showering them with gifts that have a real 'Wow!' factor.

With your support we hope to be a vehicle that blesses and enriches thousands of women's lives by showing them that we believe in them.

For more information or to nominate someone in your world, please visit our website:

www.alm.org.uk/cherishfoundation

Or contact the Abundant Life Church to request an information pack on: +44 (0)1274 307233

By the same Author:

Consumer or Consumed:

David wrote, 'Zeal for your House consumes me.' So what about you?

In every House there are two types of people, consumers and the consumed. Over the years God's House has been given a bad reputation because it has served the consumers of church life and marginalized those with a genuine zeal.

In this challenging and insightful book, Charlotte takes a look 'through the keyhole' to explore just what we should be seeing and hearing in God's House, and shares practical wisdom to equip everyone involved in building the church today.

This book includes a specially created DVD with three video tracks demonstrating the consumed heart of the Abundant Life Church.

Further Resources:

For more information about teaching resources by Charlotte Scanlon-Gambill, Pastor Paul Scanlon or Abundant Life Music visit our on-line store at www.alm.org.uk/shop or contact:

Abundant Life Ministries
Wapping Road
Bradford
West Yorkshire
BD3 OEQ

Tel: +44 (0) 1274 307233
Fax: +44 (0) 1274 740698
e-mail: admin@alm.org.uk